Thinking
LIKE A GENERALIST

Thinking
LIKE A GENERALIST

Skills for Navigating a Complex World

ANGELA M. KOHNEN AND E. WENDY SAUL

PORTSMOUTH, NEW HAMPSHIRE

Stenhouse Publishers
www.stenhouse.com

Library of Congress Cataloging-in-Publication Data
Names: Kohnen, Angela M., author. | Saul, Wendy, author.
Title: Thinking like a generalist : skills for making sense of a complex world / Angela M. Kohnen and Wendy Saul.
Description: Portsmouth, New Hampshire : Stenhouse Publishers, 2020. | Includes bibliographical references and index. |
Identifiers: LCCN 2019040334 (print) | LCCN 2019040335 (ebook) | ISBN 9781625311061 (paperback) | ISBN 9781625311078 (ebook)
Subjects: LCSH: Literacy—Study and teaching. | Language arts—Correlation with content subjects. | Information literacy.
Classification: LCC LC149 .K67 2020 (print) | LCC LC149 (ebook) | DDC 302.2244—dc23
LC record available at https://lccn.loc.gov/2019040334
LC ebook record available at https://lccn.loc.gov/2019040335

Cover design, interior design, and typesetting by Cindy Butler

Manufactured in the United States of America

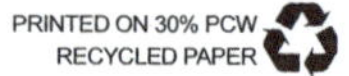

26 25 24 23 22 21 20 9 8 7 6 5 4 3 2 1

With thanks to Alan R. Newman, scientist, editor, teacher, and expert generalist.

CONTENTS

FOREWORD

I wish *Thinking Like a Generalist* had existed when I was growing up. Looking back, I realize I had the heart of a generalist from the time I took my first book out of the school library in first grade. I went right to the nonfiction shelf and grabbed *What Is a Butterfly?* After that, I just wanted to find out more—about butterflies, birds, trees, frogs. I was hooked on learning about the world. If my teachers had this book back then, I would have developed the skills of a generalist early on. That would have made me so happy, and it would have served me well as a writer and a grown-up human being.

What does it mean to be a generalist? As a writer, one of the most exciting parts of my job is doing research. As a person, my favorite thing is asking questions. In both spheres, I love to know things.

As Wendy Saul and Angela Kohnen show, we all research every day, and we also receive information every day, in different ways. I realized right away, reading Chapter 1, that the way I research in my work life is not different from how I research in my personal life. I ask questions. I look for answers. I use many different resources—people, primary sources, secondary sources. I interview, I search online, I check out books and magazines. I observe. I listen. I am a generalist. I follow paths that I choose and paths that choose me. I revel in the process of finding out, and I'm always discovering new ways to do so. That's what being a generalist means, and that's why I'm so excited this book exists for today's teachers and children.

I feel very strongly that students should learn how to research generally, not just to write a paper about a certain topic. By giving students the skills of a generalist—by learning from Saul and Kohnen's research and suggestions—you will be equipping them with the tools for their whole lives, no matter what the technology is by the time they reach adulthood.

In my role as a writer who comes into contact with schoolchildren across the country, I've talked to teachers about my research process. And teachers have asked my advice. So I share my process and suggest ways to adapt it for their students. What

I've told teachers for years is very much in sync with this book. Just as Saul and Kohnen suggest, I brainstorm (both alone and with friends and colleagues), I read texts critically, I watch myself reacting to different sources. And I let myself wander when researching.

When I talk to teachers, I suggest they consider removing the writing part from a research project. Not forever, not always, but sometimes. I suggest, especially when first introducing children to research, that they don't have them write up what they find out. Why? Because we all know what happens when a child is told to research a topic and then write about it. I remember it well. I would pull out a volume of the *World Book Encyclopedia,* find the article I needed, and then "put it into my own words." What did that teach me about research? Not very much.

So if you treat research as a skill in and of itself, you give children the skills to research any topic and to think of research as an enjoyable activity they will engage in forever.

With *Thinking Like a Generalist,* you will help your students understand and become lifelong learners—the greatest gift of all.

—Deborah Heiligman

Deborah Heiligman is the author of over thirty books for children and young adults. *Vincent and Theo: The Van Gogh Brothers* won the Boston Globe-Horn Book Award for nonfiction, the YALSA Excellence in Nonfiction Award, the SCBWI Golden Kite Award, and the ALA Printz Honor. *Charles and Emma: The Darwins' Leap of Faith* also won the YALSA Excellence in Nonfiction Award and the Printz Honor and was a National Book Award finalist. For more information visit www.DeborahHeiligman.com.

ACKNOWLEDGMENTS

It is better to know some of the questions
than all of the answers.

—JAMES THURBER

The questions at the heart of this book were discussed and refined over many years. Joining us, either knowingly or sometimes just in print or online, were journalists, librarians, children's book authors, civic activists, disciplinary experts, and, of course, teachers. They are our models. They also formed the ideas we sought to synthesize or juxtapose with one another. Our special thanks to Jeanne Reardon whose teacher and generalist wisdom always enlightened these conversations.

Speaking of teachers, we wish to thank those who tried out or initiated the lessons featured here. A big thank-you to the teacher participants in the National Science Foundation–funded project "Science Literacy Through Science Journalism," as well as students from University of Florida who participated in Angela's online class. The University of Missouri–St. Louis (UMSL) graduate group that named themselves the "SaulStars" also provided support and critical feedback. Help with specific lessons was offered by Marsha Buerger, Scott Krazner, Rob Lamb, Carrie Launius, Jon Mundorf, Ruth Nathan, and Inda Schaenen. We hope that their insights into what works when, with whom, and under what circumstances are properly reflected in the pages that follow.

Institutional support for this work was generously provided by the UMSL, Springboard to Learning, and the University of Florida. Thank you also to Gillian E. Mertens, research assistant extraordinaire.

Angela's own children, Cecilia and Addie, always provided an "out-of-school" perspective on how what we are calling generalist literacy made or did not make sense.

This book only came into being because of the support and critical friendship of Toby Gordon and then later, Dan Tobin. Thank you both for your belief that there were, in fact, ideas worth developing and a book worth writing.

Part I

THE CASE FOR GENERALIST LITERACY

What does it mean to teach students to be lifelong learners? How can we prepare the students in our classrooms for a future that we can't yet imagine? These are two of the questions that led us to write this book. They are also the questions that we have been asking ourselves, each other, and the teachers and students with whom we work for over a decade. During this time, we've witnessed changes in the way people access information, the development of new technologies and gadgets, and a seemingly endless stream of news stories about misinformation and propaganda. We've also worked with teachers who have encouraged students' curiosities and used authentic student interests as an avenue for teaching a new kind of literacy: generalist literacy.

In the pages that follow, we'll define generalist literacy and make the case that it belongs in school. Generalist literacy is the kind of literacy that will support students long after they leave our classrooms, providing them with skills and dispositions to navigate a complex health question, debunk a conspiracy theory, make a wise consumer decision, or investigate a political issue.

To make this book easier to work with, we have color-coded various sections of the text:

- light blue for classroom vignettes;
- dark blue for classroom-ready activities;
- light green for activities you, the reader, can complete;
- and light orange for elaborated definitions or explanations of information you might need.

Navigating the information landscape can be a challenge. If we want our students to be lifelong learners, we have to give them access to the tools and practices they will need to move confidently through this sometimes-treacherous terrain. In the next few chapters, you'll meet the generalist, an expert information navigator, who can serve as a model for you and your students.

Chapter 1

MEET THE GENERALIST

Consider for a moment all of the information you encountered last week. Chances are that you actively sought out some of the following—a recipe for dinner, directions to an event, details relevant to an upcoming election issue, reviews of products or restaurants or movies, and perhaps an answer to a health or technical question. Maybe you were taking a class and had to prepare for a discussion or an exam. Some of what came to your attention may have entered your life practically against your will, via the news station that was on in the car mechanic's waiting room or a flyer that was stuck in your mailbox. And some of it may have come to you through sources you regularly count on and access deliberately (television channels or newspaper websites, a friend's social media account, the local paper), even if you weren't looking for a specific piece of information.

Though their taste may differ from your own, this same busy and tempting menu of information surrounds students. How might schools help young people become more thoughtful and articulate in their responses to real-world information today? As teachers we also need to ask a different question: Given the changes that will occur in both content and delivery, what can we teach today about information that will be of use ten or fifteen years after high school graduation? This book is designed to help answer those questions.

We call our approach to real-world information *generalist literacy*, a term borrowed from Lewis Mumford's concept of the "generalist" (1961). Mumford was himself a generalist, working at times as a historian, architect, city planner, literary critic, and writer. Mumford likens a generalist to a trader, someone who pieces together information and experiences from their travels, exchanging goods and ideas among those who live and work in silos. Generalist literacy represents a stance; even specialists sometimes need to put on their generalist hats.

Generalist literacy is what we use when working outside our specialist fields or areas of competence. For example, a chemist uses generalist thinking when trying to understand geology or how to comfort her colicky baby. A historian uses generalist thinking when trying to determine why tomatoes won't grow in his garden. Sometimes generalist interests can lead to specialist knowledge: Dan started off as someone with an interest in food and became an extraordinarily talented pastry chef.

Generalists have a deep regard for the work of specialists, but generalists aren't always striving to *become* specialists themselves. Instead, the generalist derives energy, insight, and satisfaction from gathering, comparing, analyzing, and synthesizing information. Generalist literacy is what you do as you make decisions about both important and less important issues—everything from whether to go through with a medical procedure to choosing a new restaurant for a special occasion. Sometimes a generalist search for information is stimulated by a question (How should the school library spend its limited funds?), and sometimes the information gathering is triggered by an observation or a curiosity (this fourth grader isn't really reading, although he is a great storyteller). A generalist's imagination might be stirred by something they encountered incidentally, from an article a friend sent or a snippet of a television show seen in a waiting room.

The information gathered in a generalist mode can be thought of as existing on a continuum (see Figure 1.1), with intentional (or actively sought after) information on one end and incidental (or passively received) information on the other. In between is "semi-incidental" information, information encountered because you actively went to a particular source, though you didn't seek the exact information you acquired. We think of these semi-incidental information sources as something like the salons or coffeehouses of old—a "space" (usually not physical) where you deliberately place yourself to find out about interesting things, even if you don't know ahead of time what those things might be.

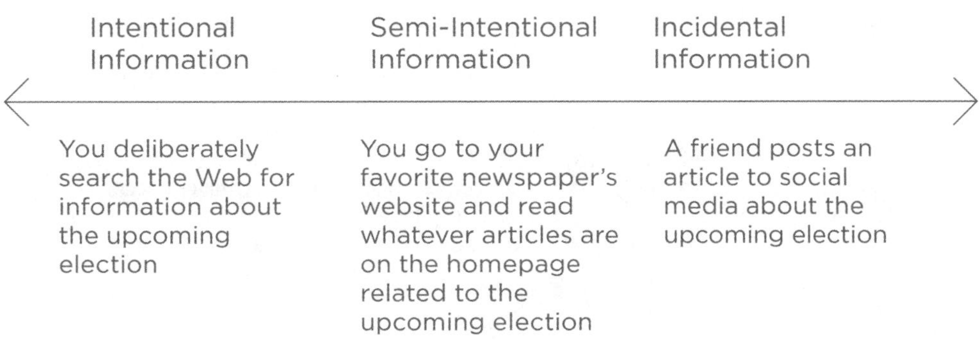

Figure 1.1 How Active Was the Information Consumer?

Adapted from: Kohnen, Angela M., and E. Wendy Saul. 2018. "Information Literacy in the Internet Age: Making Space for Students' Intentional and Incidental Knowledge." *Journal of Adolescent and Adult Literacy, 61: 671–679.*

We find this continuum helpful in thinking about what teachers can do to support students as critical consumers and generalists. Begin by considering the information opportunities evident in the classrooms in which you work. Where do these information opportunities sit on the continuum? How much comes directly from the curriculum and how much from you? How much from your students or their families? How much from information encountered via the media? As you work with this book, use your initial responses as a kind of baseline. Where are the opportunities to bring in information from students' lived experiences? From current events? From the community?

What Were You Looking for, Anyway?

Use the continuum in Figure 1.1 to think about your own information encounters. Make a list of your intentional information searches. What kinds of things do you seek out? How do you know where to go for information? How do you decide when to stop? When (and why) do you find yourself down a wormhole? What means, other than the Internet, do you use to access information intentionally?

Now consider the incidental information you encounter. What kinds of things "found you"? How? How often does this occur online? What about offline? When does incidental information inspire you to go on an intentional search?

Finally, think about the middle area. What do you learn incidentally because you have intentionally put yourself in a particular space? Consider radio stations, newspapers, magazines, frequently visited websites, social media groups, libraries, bookstores, and so on. How did you decide these were good spaces to hang out in to learn something incidentally? What criteria do you use? What role does browsing (both physically, by flipping through a magazine or wandering through the library aisles, as well as virtually, by scrolling through social media posts within your favorite groups) play in your life? And which information sources do you purposefully not access? Why?

This continuum leads us to certain understandings:

1. To be an intentional information seeker, students need *skills* to seek out and sort through text.
2. To manage the overwhelming information that they encounter incidentally, students need a second set of *skills*, different skills perhaps than those they need to do well with school tasks that typically focus on intentional exploration.
3. To think carefully about the sources of semi-incidental information they access, students need a third set of *understandings*.

A number of excellent books focus on the left side of the continuum—how to research a topic or how teachers might align more closely with state standards.

This book, however, focuses on the way that incidental and semi-incidental information—the stuff on the right side of the continuum that pervades and becomes a significant part of our lives—might become or even create interests that can serve as the basis for schoolwork. We also seek to explore and foster the relationship between the production and consumption of ideas, how the right side and left side of the continuum connect for students as readers, writers, and thoughtful citizens.

APPROACHES TO TEACHING INFORMATION LITERACY

For more than fifty years schools have focused on content-area literacy (previously known as content-area reading). The goal of this approach is to provide students with strategies to better comprehend and retain ideas they encounter in textbook-like material. To this end, an alphabet salad of mnemonics has been designed to help with this task: SQ3R, KWL, Frayer Model, and so on. Graphic organizers are also recognized as effective ways to help students sort through and take notes on important ideas.

Underlying each of the strategies for organizing information, and posing and answering questions, is an assumption that the skills needed to read textbooks and text-support materials do not come naturally to all young people. When explicitly taught, these strategies have helped students, especially struggling students, read and write more effectively and do better in school.

For example, Ms. Ortiz tells her class to first scan the chapter, looking at text features like bolded headings and captions under photographs and charts. "What do you think this chapter will be about?" probes the teacher. "And what do you know or think you know about this topic?" she goes on, taking notes on a piece of chart paper that will be used later to check earlier understandings against newfound information from their schoolbook. We all know the drill—and it's not really a bad drill at all.

For the past ten years (if not longer) teachers have felt the push to add more informational text to the reading diets of students. The hope, one we surely share, is that these changes may help prepare young people for the demands of college and career and enable them to do well on their standardized tests. Partly in response to the global approach that underpins content literacy instruction, and partly in response to the call for college and career readiness, educators have begun pointing to disciplinary literacy as an important contributor to student learning. Interestingly, two groups use the term *disciplinary*. The first focuses primarily on the literacy end of disciplinary literacy and distinguishes disciplinary literacy skills from basic literacy skills (e.g., decoding and becoming comfortable reading high-frequency words) and intermediate literacy skills (generic comprehension).

Disciplinary literacy experts hope teachers offer specific instruction to address the specialized vocabulary and forms used by historians, scientists, mathematicians, and others. Instead of talking about floating and sinking, learners are introduced to and expected to use terms like *Archimedes' principle*, *displacement*, *buoyancy*, and *density*. They are taught to recognize and use such vocabulary in conversation and in the texts they create and are tested on. This view of literacy learning is often drawn as a pyramid with basic literacy as the base, intermediate literacy as the middle, and disciplinary literacy as the apex, indicating both a hierarchy of difficulty as well as the amount of time dedicated to basic, intermediate, and disciplinary teaching.

The other reference to discipline-based literacy comes from scholars associated with "structure of the disciplines," an idea best represented by the work of Jerome Bruner. In his now classic work, *The Process of Education* (1976), Bruner graphically represents curriculum as a spiral rather than as the top of a literacy pyramid. He begins with what still rings as a radical statement: "Any subject can be taught effectively in some intellectually honest form to any child at any stage of development." For example, in a curriculum he and colleagues designed in the 1970s, *Man: A Course of Study (MACOS)*, Bruner begins by introducing the relatively simple life cycle of the salmon, builds to increasingly complex organisms from the herring gull to the baboon, and ends his spiral with observations and information about the life cycle and activities of the Netsilik Inuit. Young people are asked, through Bruner's curriculum, to think about what it means to be human, which behaviors are innate to our species, and which behaviors are learned. Bruner was more concerned with developmental appropriateness and intuitive and analytical thinking than with vocabulary and career readiness.

However you define *disciplinary literacy*, though, at its root it is about preparing young people for more and more specialized ways of thinking about knowledge. Generalist literacy, on the other hand, seeks to support reasoning and critical thinking relevant to everyday decision making—often about topics about which we have no specialized understanding or knowledge. In that sense, generalist literacy is intrinsically motivational because it builds on recognized personal interests about issues beyond school and work.

IMPORTANCE AND PREPAREDNESS

Let's return to something more current, the topics that you, the reader, sought to gather information on and learn about in the past week, especially what you read online or gathered through the media. How many of those daily encounters—the things you really took time to look up and learn more about—have to do with your academic work or your career? Some, that's for sure, but certainly not all. Though schools are and should be concerned with college and career readiness, we recognize that the daily information needs of adults are not primarily related to academics or even career in nature. Instead, let's think about people's information needs in terms of two variables: *importance* (Is the information need high stakes or low stakes?) and *preparation* (How well has your education and/or experience prepared you to deal with the information you find?) (see Figure 1.2).

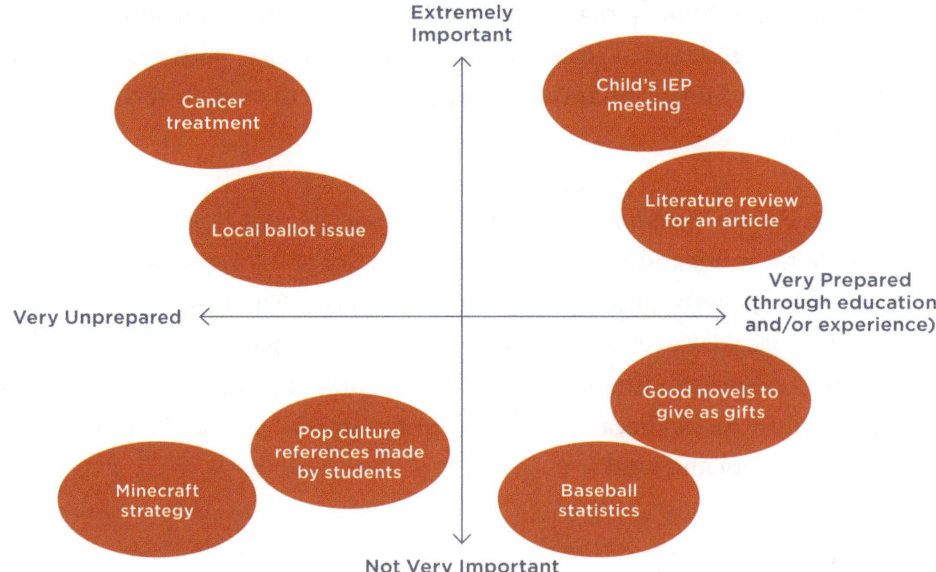

Figure 1.2: Preparation and Importance as Variables Impacting Information Seeking

Note: Examples are from Angela's perspective.

Is It Important?

Use the graphic in Figure 1.2 to think about your own recent information-seeking endeavors. What do you put in each quadrant? Try asking a friend or a student how their searches differ from yours.

Does the starting point for your information seeking differ, depending on what quadrant you are in? What about your time investment? Your interest in verifying information?

INFORMATION SEEKING IN SCHOOLS

Here is the question we pose: What role should schools play in preparing students to find and better understand the different kinds of information they will need as adults? In all likelihood, educators see the low-stakes searches as low priority for schools; perhaps teachers might model how they engage in low-stakes searches of different kinds (Why are tennis balls yellow?), but otherwise these kinds of searches probably demand little curricular space. Moreover, we all probably agree that the high-stakes searches should be a high priority for schools, even if they aren't part of the curriculum.

At present it seems that the information-seeking instruction focuses almost exclusively on preparing students for searches that fall into the upper right quadrant. In excellent classrooms, these searches and accompanying instruction might even take on a disciplinary literacy lens, wherein students are exposed to particular websites that historians (or scientists or mathematicians) find highly credible and, at the same time, expose learners to a new disciplinary vocabulary and rhetorical style. That's important work—no doubt about it.

However, our call for generalist literacy encourages educators to pay more attention to the upper left quadrant—the high-stakes/low-preparation kinds of searches. After all, the upper left quadrant is where our most confounding adult questions fall. Should I buy a home or rent? If I buy, what kind of mortgage should I take out? What should I do about my child's disruptive school behavior: counseling? A new school? How should I vote on an upcoming state solar energy initiative?

Generalist literacy instruction is designed to help learners navigate the world of informational text—especially online text—as we try to make sense of important issues for which we have had little academic preparation. How do we prepare students to deal with these kinds of questions, and, even more important perhaps, how do we help them to make sense of the informational texts they find?

With all the attention schools pay to opinion and argument writing, it is surprising how little time most schools dedicate to engaging students with questions that fall into the upper left quadrant of Figure 1.2 (high importance, low preparation). Instead, we see countless examples of students being asked to provide textual evidence drawn from presupplied articles regarding their opinions on such topics as: Should the United States get rid of the penny? Should you strive for neatness in your room, or is it okay to be a little messy? Should students be required to engage in extracurricular activities? What should be done to control the wild horse population in the West?

Our guess is that such questions are designed to serve as a proxy for those upper left-hand questions—sort of real life, but not based on the real life of most people we know. Although any one of these questions might provoke interest and curiosity in some students, the majority of people do not authentically engage with these mandated queries. Recognizing that student writers won't write well unless they *are* engaged, some teachers dedicate class time to helping students connect with the prompt—a completely schoolish skill that has very little utility outside of classrooms.

We've also watched excellent teachers tell students to skim through presupplied articles quickly and pick the side of an argument that is easiest to write about (and *easiest* is defined not as the side with the most compelling evidence, but the side where evidence can be marshaled as quickly as possible by the student writer)—there is no time, the teachers point out, for thinking about the issue and evidence when a multi-paragraph essay must be created on the spot. Though the teachers we know wish it were otherwise, in many districts the move toward more nonfiction texts in schools often becomes lesson after lesson to support better test scores, with any other rationale swept away in the wake of standardized testing.

A CLOSER LOOK AT INFORMATIONAL TEXT

In schools, information seeking is generally tied to printed passages, even when the topic calls for real-world, timely conclusions. Moreover, the texts are typically preselected based on reading scores or curricular fit. In an attempt to encourage close reading, have we as educators overshot the mark, privileging school-selected texts over other sources of knowledge? Are we ignoring the fact that all of us are best served when engaged in authentic, challenging conversation? Has real-world, critical thinking been shoved to the back seat or perhaps even the trunk to make room for the close reading of prescribed texts? From a generalist perspective, we question whether relevant knowledge resides in any one text alone, and especially in prechosen texts.

Consider this example designed to prepare primary students for the Common Core State Standards (CCSS) (Achieve the Core). Here the teacher is directed to present a text that describes why Ann likes dogs and the narrator likes cats.

> I told Ann that cats are better pets because they are clean, quiet, and very cute. Cats wash themselves with their tongues. You don't have to walk them. They use a litter box. Also cats are sweet and quiet. I think dogs are too noisy! They bark a lot. They don't clean themselves or use a litter box. Dogs need someone to give them baths, train them, and walk them. Dogs are more work.

Ann then makes her case for dogs—they are better friends, and so on. Before being asked to address the prompt—"Which pet is the right (sometimes written as 'best') one for you?"—students are told to brainstorm with a partner and take notes on the subject from their reading.

A real-world answer to this prompt—which pet is best—might include information from the text, and might not. Unfortunately, most tests (and the curriculum designed to prepare students for these tests) privilege textual evidence above all else. We argue that students are better prepared for their real-world information needs through activities that invite them to make connections and gather their own information. What if the child lives in a no-pet apartment, has a mom who is allergic to cats, has no money for pet food, or wants a rabbit or a goldfish? How does real-world experience enter this picture or become valued in the school context?

As students work their way through the grades, text sets continue to be preselected and citations to these specific readings are expected to show up in students' argumentative or informational responses. Again, the predetermined text may make sense if a teacher is seeking an example for a think-aloud or wishes to practice a particular approach to information searching, but close reading turns into a mere exercise if no opportunity to apply understandings to authentic sources of information is apparent. Close informational reading becomes merely a schoolish exercise when it is not tied to the world beyond school.

Ultimately, we as teachers want to choose topics of personal interest and help students find and assess information on their own. Kids come to school with a variety of experiences that should serve them well as researchers. The final insult may be yet to come: if and when students are asked to do research, school Internet filters often block much of what's available on the Web, and assignment rules (e.g., "Include at least two books and two Internet sources") may further restrict information sources and preclude students from using their outside knowledge.

For all practical purposes, students in schools are often asked to live inside a bubble of controlled or protected information. Instead of attending to information from the outside world or talking about information that students encounter in their day-to-day lives, we often end up managing, controlling, and approving of what students read and write in school. In this bubble, students may be asked to engage with intellectually stimulating topics or passages and they might even emerge well prepared for college classwork, but they certainly aren't ready for the nonfiction demands of adult life. As Paulo Freire cautioned well before the days of the Internet, "The basic question in school is how *NOT to separate reading the word and reading the world,* reading the text and reading the context" (1985, 20, emphasis added). Yet, in the twenty-first century, when the world is easily accessible with the click of a button or the swipe of a finger, it is shocking how much effort schools spend trying to separate curricular activities from real-world practices and information.

For students whose experiences and backgrounds align with that of the school, the predetermined curriculum may seem less problematic. Life inside the bubble and life outside the bubble look very much alike. Surely some families sit down at the dinner table and discuss the amount of money allocated to the space program or other topics likely to find their way into the school curriculum. But what about students whose nonschool lives differ markedly in funds of knowledge (e.g., Moll et al. 1992) or practices from those identified as important by the school? Is there a place for their experiences and concerns in our institutions?

Think back to the example of the required essay on which pet is best. Wouldn't it be likely that a child whose parents are considering buying a cat or dog would do much better on that essay than someone who, for instance, is experiencing homelessness? Children who see themselves regularly represented in the curriculum—because they share race, gender, geography, or religion with the figures or authors mandated for study—may find that the curriculum feels less incidental or unfamiliar than those who rarely see themselves represented in curricular materials.

Our goal in this book is to offer a framework for thinking about the current information environment and propose a closer look at the skills you, and other adults who can serve well as models, employ when searching for information. Generalist thinking involves both expanding and narrowing. It encourages wandering and may, at times, be inefficient. It encourages students to find resources that make sense in terms of the subject at hand and for various stakeholders who are impacted by that subject in terms of the technologies and opportunities for conversation that currently define their lives. Our hope is that generalist literacy bridges the divide between the skills needed to navigate the information landscape in schools and the skills needed to successfully do so in the real world.

Chapter 2

PROMOTING A GENERALIST IDENTITY

Our guess is that you already know plenty of generalists. These are people who read widely and thoughtfully. They ask good questions. In the language of the Wild West, they don't "shoot from the hip." Interview them. We did just that. How did they go about researching a topic? From what evidence did they derive their opinions? Not surprisingly, the expert generalists we studied embodied certain attitudes and perspectives as well as ways of doing their work. They had a kind of generalist identity, a way that they thought about themselves as problem-solvers.

We took our lead from researchers and curriculum developers of the 1960s who started by looking at what real scientists did day in and day out. They wanted young people not only to do what scientists do but also to think like scientists and identify as scientists. As a result, students were invited to observe carefully, make notes about phenomena, ask questions, and sort and analyze data. In classrooms, students adjusted ramps, covered them with various materials, and practiced sending balls of different sizes and textures down those ramps. It was a radical, perhaps even exhilarating, way of thinking about developing curriculum. However, for the many teachers of that era for whom teaching science was reading the science textbook, this change may have felt strange and out of control.

A similar attention to expertise led to new writing curricula in the 1980s. As a result, teacher educators like Donald Graves and those who followed in his wake—Lucy Calkins, Nancie Atwell, and Carol Berkenkotter, among others—learned from the habits of practicing authors. These authors were quoted regularly in classrooms as a way of inspiring young writers and readers and helping them to figure their way through texts of various kinds. Using author insights, literacy teachers were able to offer minilessons about the choices real writers make, which in turn helped readers think about text as the result of author intent and author choice. Similar efforts to examine the processes engaged in by historians or artists or even athletes have changed the way the best schools now go about teaching history, art, and physical education.

The luckiest students work under the guidance of teachers who have themselves engaged in the doing of science, history, art, and writing. These teachers not only have learned the techniques and strategies of the experts but more importantly, perhaps, have been immersed in the more subtle aspects of practice including perspective taking, timing, and appreciating what experts value. Authenticity is key; people who build curriculum from observing practitioners avoid activities that exist only in classrooms.

EXPERT GENERALISTS

Like the folks who studied scientists or writers, we set out to learn about generalists from meeting and talking with them. Three questions guided our research: What does it mean to be a competent generalist? How do generalists do their work? And what can we learn from generalists that we can take back to the classroom?

The generalists we interviewed and learned from—largely journalists, children's nonfiction authors, and librarians, as well as others whose work lives involve bringing together information from multiple, credible sources—displayed certain attitudes. We believe three of these attitudes are essential to cultivate in schools:

- Curiosity
- Open-minded skepticism
- Persistence

Modeling the Generalist Behavior

You probably already begin the school year articulating the attitudes and values you want students to demonstrate in your classroom: respect, kindness, responsibility, and so on. Successfully teaching generalist literacy depends on a similar kind of attitude seeding.

Just as you spend time developing routines that promote respect and classroom community, you can begin your year with routines that can sow the seeds of generalist literacy. Here are some examples:

- Share your real-life questions and curiosities with students. If you have an interesting example of looking for and finding good information, tell students. Over time, they may begin sharing their own examples.
- Make your go-to sources of incidental information public by referencing them ("I heard a really interesting story yesterday on NPR news") as appropriate. Just hearing about high-quality sources of information can be valuable.
- Look at local news or subject-specific news headlines together as a class. Some teachers find it easiest to pick a day—Friday, maybe—where class starts with news reading.
- Model the key characteristics of a generalist—curiosity, skepticism, and persistence—through your own behavior. This may involve developing a set of questions you can ask students (and yourself) as appropriate. For example:
    - "I wonder how they know that. Who did the research?"
    - "I wonder how big of a deal this is. How could I find out?"
    - "This isn't really the information I was looking for. What's another way I could search?"

Naming and promoting the generalist personal attributes, dispositions, or identities may begin as early as preschool and continue through college; as college instructors we still remind students of their importance. The good news is that these values can be embedded in almost any lesson or curriculum. Even when working with the most rigid teaching materials, there is room to support the development of curiosity, open-minded skepticism, and a practical persistence.

CURIOSITY

Curiosity, as we use the term, involves wondering, asking questions, and looking for answers, often across a range of fields and topics. Expert generalists aren't necessarily better than others at memorizing facts or identifying sources, but they can't imagine being alive without learning for learning's sake. Expert generalists are not afraid of querying experts or looking dumb. On the contrary, they are anxious to assuage their curiosity and tie new information to old. They feel especially satisfied when they can play ideas against one another to develop a more informed perspective. The writers we interviewed see themselves as a proxy for their readers—finding answers to questions their readers didn't even know that they had. They love learning and presenting information that their audience would find so interesting or delicious they would anxiously read more.

As humans we start our lives being curious—young children typically ask twenty-five to fifty questions a day when at home, says Susan Engel (2015), author of *The Hungry Mind: The Origins of Curiosity in Children*. But when they get to school—perhaps because of the social pace and space of the classroom—that number drops to one to three questions. Generalist literacy celebrates curiosity—wanting to know more and feeling that we can meaningfully address our questions. Generalist literacy is what enables us to scratch the curiosity itch. So, what can we do in classrooms to keep that curiosity alive and growing?

Engel, an experimental psychologist, designed an experiment to learn more about how a teacher's goals and actions affect student behavior. In her study, a teacher and student met in a room packed with science equipment and worked through an activity often called "dancing raisins." A few raisins are tossed into a glass of carbonated water, the bubbles collect on the raisins' wrinkled sides, and when enough bubbles collect, the raisins float to the top of the glass. As the bubbles pop at the top, the raisins fall again to the bottom of the glass, producing the "dance."

With half of her student "subjects," about halfway through the activity the teacher said something like, "Hey, I wonder what would happen if we tried this with a candy instead of the raisin" and dropped a Skittle into the glass. With other students, about halfway through the teacher stopped and said something like, "Let's tidy up this area" and started to clean things. In each case, the teacher then left the room: "I have to go away for a few minutes. Feel free to do whatever you want."

What happened? The children whose teacher showed curiosity continued to play with materials and learn. The children whose teacher cleaned up simply stood there and waited for the teacher to return. The lesson here is undeniable: what teachers think and do and say matters.

Engel's work involved science materials, but the same principles may apply to learning from texts. These are questions to ask about life in our classroom:

1. Are we offering students the time and tools to help figure things out for themselves?

2. Are we naming the values (like curiosity, skepticism, and persistence) we wish to promote?

3. Have we designed a physical space that encourages exploration and independent curiosity? What materials—texts, the Internet, and realia—are available for students to use to investigate their own questions?

4. Have we developed minilessons that promote these values?

Promoting Curiosity

- Create a question board where students can post their queries and other students can respond to them. At intervals (every other Friday?) sort the questions with your students: Which can be answered through one source, and which would do better with multiple sources? Which questions do students find most compelling, and why? Where did this curiosity come from? Who might you want to interview to help scratch this curiosity itch?
- Create a shelf for displaying interesting objects. These can include both natural objects (e.g., sea beans) or engineered objects (e.g., antique tools). The shelf can be a place to inspire curiosity or could be used for more specific questions (e.g., "What's the function of . . . ?"). (See Appendix A for more ideas.)
- Invite students to jot down their curiosities and put them into a fishbowl. Choose one each day as a "bell ringer." Are these testable questions? How might you go about figuring out a position in regard to them?
- Celebrate student curiosity. Be sure to notice (either privately or in a more public way) students who have consistently shown an interest in learning more and extending their interests beyond school assignments and subjects. Pay special attention to those whose interests may be different from yours.
- Try to take the curiosity temperature of students in your class. Create a survey (see Appendix B for an example). Note changes and discuss results with both the student and parents in parent/teacher conferences.

OPEN-MINDED SKEPTICISM

Expert generalists approach information seeking with a desire to reach the best conclusion they can about a topic using the most current and reliable information they can access. They attempt to recognize and set aside their personal biases and emotions and, instead, work to access and understand what various stakeholders and experts say. Sometimes expert generalists rely only on primary (or original) sources of information. The expert generalists we know who work with historical topics often fall into this category, relying on primary sources—diaries, letters, newspaper articles—as much as they can, avoiding any secondary sources or other historical interpretations of events until very late in their research process. However, when expert generalists are exploring incredibly complex or specialized topics (especially scientific issues), they must also rely on guides, both human and published, and on the interpretations of experts (see Chapter 7 for more about types of sources). In these situations, expert generalists look for consensus among experts in the field. Even if they do not agree with the consensus, they feel a need to understand and refer to expert opinion. When no consensus exists, they try to understand the nuances of the disagreements rather than throw up their hands or create a false dichotomy. They want to understand if this is settled science (or settled interpretations of historical events) or if current ideas are considered in flux. They evaluate and monitor outside information as well as how confident they feel about the information they encounter; they question their own understandings of issues and opinions. (For important topics, expert generalists know that a single source of information is never enough.) Yet they are not skeptical just to play devil's advocate; when they have read and understood enough credible information, they are willing to stop searching and accept what they've learned. At the same time, they also understand that for very important issues and for information in flux, it's important to stay engaged with a topic. Expert opinions evolve over time, and *credible* isn't equivalent with *true for all time*.

Open-minded skepticism may be more important now than ever. The amount of information we—and our students—consume each day continues to rise, with much of it of questionable quality. Being an open-minded skeptic means viewing all information critically—and having the skills to fact-check anything important. We once worked in a classroom where a young man asserted that Mountain Dew could prevent pregnancy. We've also met highly educated adults who believe the chemtrails left by jet planes are part of a government conspiracy. Such assertions provide the perfect opportunity to model the kinds of questions generalists ask when confronted with questionable assertions (see "Promoting Open-Minded Skepticism" box on page 24).

Promoting Open-Minded Skepticism

To teach open-minded skepticism, present students with assertions: "Glucosamine will help with arthritis." "LeBron James is the greatest basketball player of all time." "Raising the minimum wage would cost teenagers important summer job opportunities." Help students learn to recognize assertions and ask the following kinds of questions:

- "Who says? What is his or her expertise on or connection to the topic?"
- "What criteria were used to make this assertion? Could other criteria have been used?"
- "Do experts generally agree, or is there some debate?"
- "Is this the newest thinking on this subject, or are ideas still in flux?"

For older students, invite them to list three assertions they find on the social media they read. Bring them to class and interrogate the students, using the questions here and others that you generate together.

Classroom Cover-Up

Ethical dilemmas are another opportunity for exploring open-minded skepticism—and they come up frequently in schools. We worked in a school where students were casually talking about the boys' wrestling team, a favorite for the state title.

"They use makeup on their legs and stuff," one student remarked.

The teacher was startled. "They do what?"

Several students nodded. "Makeup. To cover up infections. You can't wrestle if you have certain skin infections—they can spread, you know?"

The teacher hadn't heard of this issue—and was surprised at how matter-of-fact his students were. He used the conversation as an opportunity to help the students generate questions: Is there a rule against fighting with skin infections? Why? Is the infection in question contagious? Are different skin conditions treated differently by the rules (i.e., MRSA versus eczema)? Do coaches know about students covering up infections? What is the punishment if they are caught? What is the motive for the players to cover up their infections (beyond just being able to participate)?

When teaching open-minded skepticism, we recommend choosing topics about which students (1) already know something and (2) are interested in learning more. It's hard to begin with an overly complex or incredibly controversial topic—students will have a difficult time comprehending information they read or they will have entrenched beliefs that are hard to disrupt. This doesn't mean controversial and complex topics aren't important—of course they are!—but they don't make good topics for first introducing open-mindedness. If you happen to overhear your students debating a conspiracy theory or an urban legend, take advantage of the teachable moment. You may also choose to visit a fact-checking website to help students learn how professional fact-checkers examine stories. Be sure you are visiting an actual fact-checking website and not a satirical one, and always preview the stories first (the content on fact-checking websites may not be appropriate for your students). The Poytner Institute keeps track of fact-checking websites from all over the world that have agreed to abide by a set of core principles. You can read about the core principles and see the list of fact-checking organizations by searching for the International Fact-Checking Network or visiting https://ifcncodeofprinciples.poynter.org/signatories.

PERSISTENCE

Much has been written recently about the importance of resilience and grit. Just as resilience and persistence in a sport require practice and honing of specific skills and behaviors, so does the kind of persistence that is useful to generalists. The generalists to whom we talked use the notion of persistence in four ways.

1. They are **persistent in slogging through difficult, often technical material.** This could include technical specs to decide which car was better for their purposes, legal filings, or financial documents. Whatever the text, they pushed themselves to remain vigilant and look for the pieces of information they wanted or needed.

2. They are **persistent in self-checking**. Did they really understand what they read? Were they able to gather enough

information to convince themselves that they know what they are talking about? Do they have the evidence to convince others?

3. They **persistently and conscientiously track information**. Have they taken notes on the material they need, and can they find it again? Is it organized? Legible? Correctly cited? We don't think that any of them saw this kind of persistence as "fun," but some really liked the fact that they were good at it.

4. Finally, they all **view persistence in terms of scope and time**. The journalist who has 500 words and a midnight deadline has different constraints and thinks of persistence differently than a feature writer with up to 5,000 words due in a week or an investigative reporter who takes a year to work though a story. Necessity often guides the decisions and actions of generalists, and it often takes a kind of discipline, if not persistence, to do what needs to be done. As teachers create due dates, students need to learn to make decisions about where best to spend their limited time.

All these kinds of persistence come into play when deciding, for example, whether or not to seek the opinion of a second doctor. Have you located the right documents that describe the problem at hand? Do you understand the medical issues involved in your case? Can you go into the office with the information you need to ask your questions? And finally, do you have time for a second opinion?

Teachers tell us that when trying to encourage persistence, classroom atmosphere is critically important. "It's about relationships," says a teacher friend. "I can look at kids—because they know how much I like and respect them—and say 'This isn't bad, but I know you can do better. Keep trying.'" She goes on: "I have high expectations, and they know it."

"Model what you do when you are frustrated by informational tasks," says another educator. Pose a real problem: "I told the kids about the waiter who spilled a glass of water on my phone: Should I get a new or refurbished one? What issues do I need to consider? Cost is only one. What about the length of time before my phone contract is due for renewal? What features on the new phone matter? Camera quality? Space for downloading photos? Policy for international travel? Geographical coverage?" She models thinking aloud about the various problems this situation raises and asks students to help her think about possible questions and where to look for answers. She asks aloud, "Is this a good answer? Can I find something better? Do I want to spend the time?"

Show students that you are the kind of teacher who is curious, skeptical, and persistent. Teacher Rob Lamb tells us:

> Really, I think it all comes back to relationships. Ask them an honest question. Most questions I ask in class, and most questions teachers ask, we know the answers to—that's how teaching works. They *know* that I know the answer and the only reason they are giving me that answer is because it's attached to a grade, because they have to. There's no choice in that. They're *my* questions.
>
> I know that I do much better with them and that I teach more about curiosity, skepticism, and persistence when we are asking authentic questions of one another about something *they* care about. We've talked about things like the game *Fortnite*—and why new versions are called "seasons," which I think is really strange—or sports games or conspiracy theories they read online. They care about the answers—and are willing to spend time and effort to understand.

We are all flooded with opportunities to teach curiosity, skepticism, and persistence, in both the formal and informal moments of the school day. And yet these opportunities can easily be missed. As a kind of self-check—when driving home or folding the laundry—ask yourself what you did today to promote a generalist identity, one that regards curiosity, skepticism, and persistence as dispositions that matter in your classroom and what you might do tomorrow to keep working toward these goals.

THE READ-ALOUD-THINK-ALOUD (RATA): YOUR CHANCE TO HAVE IT ALL

As we've argued, students often experience information they encounter in the classroom as incidental or semi-incidental—it is selected by the teacher, grade-level team, district, or state—not by the student. Students may be more or less willing and prepared to engage with this information encountered in school, depending on their out-of-school lives (i.e., their community, dinner conversations, the television or other media they've been exposed to, and their previous academic experiences). All of these sources of incidental information may be consistent with what they study in school or completely at odds with it. Through the read-aloud-think-aloud (RATA), teachers demonstrate how active reading enables thinkers to connect with ideas. Teachers can also help students to move from passively receiving information to actively, *intentionally* reacting to it.

The RATA includes the following steps:

1. Select an informational text to read aloud to students.
2. Ideally, put the text where students can see it (either project the text for students to read, hold it up, or give them copies to mark up).
3. Read the text, stopping to voice your thinking about the content.

Sounds simple, right? But, in fact, this strategy is more complex than it might first appear. And, when done well, it is one of the most powerful ways we've seen to create an environment in which students are excited to learn more about a wide range of topics.

The Read-Aloud-Think-Aloud

- Do select a text that (1) you are authentically interested in, (2) is appropriate for your students, and (3) allows you to model the generalist literacy skills you are targeting.
- Do skim the text ahead of time to get a sense of the big ideas.
- Do choose authentic texts—news (written, radio, or TV) stories or trade books rather than textbooks or materials from curriculum companies.
- Do ask questions that you have about the reading as you go (real, authentic questions that you don't know the answers to).
- Do voice your thinking as you go—make connections to previous learning or your own life, or take an interesting side trip to investigate some aspect in greater detail.
- Do use your best judgment about when to add in background information necessary for understanding. Occasionally you may need to define a word or supply information so the students can make sense of the text, but this shouldn't take up too much of the RATA. (If you find yourself doing this too much, save the text for another kind of activity.)
- Do strive for a balance between thinking and reading—don't lose the thread of the text by asking too many questions, but voice enough of your thinking so students get a glimpse inside of your mind.
- Do think about the visual elements that accompany the text (see Appendix C for more information).
- Do use the text as a springboard to intentional information seeking.

- Don't completely script and rehearse your RATA ahead of time—this can make the experience feel forced, not authentic.
- Don't use the RATA as a chance to ask comprehension questions as you read (questions like "Does anyone know what _____ means?"). The RATA is a chance to ask your *real* questions, questions you don't know the answers to.
- Don't worry if you don't know how to pronounce every word in the reading—consider this an opportunity to show how real readers make their best guesses.
- Don't avoid articles that challenge your thinking—once again, this is an opportunity to grapple in front of the students. This uncertainty won't undermine your credibility in the classroom. In fact, many students find it reassuring to see their teacher as a real person!
- Don't always read to the very end—you don't have to read every word to have an effective RATA, especially if you are reading a news story. News stories are usually written so that the most important information is frontloaded, meaning that busy readers don't have to read the last paragraphs to get the most important information.

FINDING TIME

The beauty of a RATA is that it can take very little class time and therefore can be used in those odd, leftover moments available in a school day. RATAs also can be done in nearly any content area. Teachers who examine their schedule often find a bit of time at the beginning or end of the day or right before lunch, recess, specials, or other transitions. RATAs tend to engage the entire class very quickly—a perfect activity for times that can get hectic. If you teach in an environment where students switch classes, RATAs can be a good way to start or end a class period. Teachers often make informational RATAs a regular part of the classroom routine, engaging in them daily or several times a week.

The RATA text is, of course, incidental to the students, but as you model your thinking you are also modeling your life as an intentional information seeker and consumer. Because the text is authentic—the kind of text one who is curious about the world encounters—you are showing students what it is like to be intentional about texts, or at least what it is like to be thoughtful about the texts you incidentally encounter. And, over time, students will begin suggesting or bringing in their own texts. Sometimes they may ask you to do the RATA because they're curious to hear how you think about something they found interesting. Other times, though, with your encouragement, students can lead the RATA themselves.

If you engage in regular RATAs, you will also find yourself wanting to dedicate a little more time to some readings than others. Often the RATA is short and serves as a model for students. You may conclude by brainstorming additional questions you have based on the text, but not go any further. And on the occasions you decide not to complete the entire article, tell students why you stopped: maybe it had to do with time or because you were bored, or perhaps you already learned the information you needed or found the research on which the article was based to be insufficient. Again, this is an opportunity to think aloud.

SELECTING A TEXT

What you choose to read to your students will, of course, depend on a lot of factors. Luckily, we live in an age of abundance of high-quality informational texts so the chances are good that you can find an interesting, appropriate, well-written text, no matter your context.

What you consider appropriate will depend on your goals as a teacher. We argue that the content of the reading itself matters much less than what you do with the reading. If the RATA is an opportunity to help students move from passive to active (and critical) consumers of information, then the trick is to select texts that encourage that movement. Sometimes you will choose texts that you love (or that you think students will love), and at other times you will focus on texts that are problematic.

And here's another tip. We don't suggest that teachers only choose texts that are *obviously* relevant to students (although sometimes these texts make great RATAs). RATAs can also be used to expand students' understanding of what is exciting, relevant, important, or interesting. A highly engaged teacher reading aloud a text that she finds interesting can encourage students to become interested, too, and make connections that are less than obvious to school-focused readers.

An effective RATA puts the teacher's curiosity on display and creates a culture of question asking in the classroom. For that reason, perhaps, journalistic articles are especially good for RATAs. News stories are about events in progress, the endings as yet unwritten. Teachers don't have to *pretend* to ask questions or construct meaning on the spot; a good news article forces the reader to ask questions and construct meaning.

You can find lots of news stories online that are written for upper elementary and middle school students, and the available content is constantly changing. At the time of publication, here is a short list of sources of online news stories for children:

- Time for Kids (timeforkids.com)
- Newsela (newsela.com)
- Wonderopolis (wonderopolis.org)
- Tween Tribune (tweentribune.com)

- DOGO News (dogonews.com)
- National Geographic for Kids (kids.nationalgeographic.com)
- Science News for Students (https://www.sciencenewsforstudents.org)

As students get into middle and high school, you may also choose articles written for adults. Newspapers are generally accessible to students reading at a sixth-grade level; students not able to read them independently can still follow along if the teacher is doing the reading and thinking aloud.

RATAs are a way to not only provide examples of skeptical thinking and open-mindedness but also support any content teaching you want to get in along the way. There are so many options and decisions to make: sometimes you may wish to follow your students' lead and explore the topic of a RATA in more depth because they are engaged. Other times, you may purposefully use a RATA to begin a curricular unit. And RATAs can also be useful for students looking for research topics to pursue independently. Whichever texts you choose, we've found that the RATA is the easiest way to introduce and model generalist identity throughout the school year.

A Waste of Time?

Dave was a veteran teacher who had high expectations for his students. He worried that the RATA would take too much time away from his curriculum, a curriculum he'd spent years crafting. "So, I decided to try a little experiment," he told us. "I would keep my curriculum exactly the same with one of my sections. With the other one, I would do a weekly RATA, and at the end of the semester, I'd see if there were any differences in their test scores. I was a science major—can you tell?"

Dave ended up calling off his experiment after only six weeks. "It would have been unethical not to!" he laughed. Not only were the test scores equal, but important changes were happening in his RATA classroom. Students started talking to him before and after class about the subjects he shared. Some even brought in related articles to share with their classmates. "I think they liked me better—they thought I was interesting, even kind of funny." And when he began using the RATA with his other section, the same thing happened. For Dave and many other teachers, the RATA is an opportunity to model generalist identity *and* create classroom community—in fewer than five to ten minutes of class time!

Chapter 3

DOING WHAT GENERALISTS DO

Most of us were sometimes bored, passive, apathetic school-goers, and at other times curious, open-minded, persistent learners. Many of us became teachers to help increase the appeal of learning and reduce the amount of time students spend irked and uninterested in school. We want young people to understand that the hours they spend in school have purpose in their lives outside school. We work hard to enliven the curriculum and make sure what we do in school matters to the lives of students. Generalist literacy invites these connections, helping students see that what they are learning in our classrooms matters to them today *and* in the future.

Generalist thinking is applied thinking. Sometimes it results in a product like a newspaper article or a book review, and sometimes it doesn't. Marlene, an eighth grader, kind of likes spiders but thinks that there are too many of them in her bedroom. She is interested in learning more. She begins by looking carefully: Where are they building webs? What kind of spiders are they? Are those little white balls their eggs or food that the spider caught and wrapped up? How do people get rid of spiders without poisons? How toxic are the recommended poisons? She is not trying to learn more about the species, compare spiders to other insects, or learn more about the strength of their webs. Although she has a need or desire to reduce the spider population in her bedroom, it is curiosity that fundamentally drives her search for information. Marlene wants to think about the effects of spider spray on her cats and whether the risk is worth it; her focus is not submitting a paper to her teacher.

And although Marlene's spider inquiry does not require a formal end product to be worthwhile, working toward a specific goal can be interesting for many students. Students in Dr. Marsha Buerger's seventh-grade class, for example, are excited to submit articles for an online science newspaper, *Scijourner* (scijourner.org). Dr. Buerger loves the fact that her students will learn about journalistic writing and values. She loves that they explore an important topic of their own choosing. Her seventh-grade students are clearly motivated by publication.

Whether or not students seek to create a product, there are three steps, three recursive processes, that generalists regularly employ:

- Orienting
- Sourcing
- Synthesizing

ORIENTING

The generalists with whom we talked began each study by orienting themselves. Before they moved forward in their quest to home in on information, they assessed their relationship to it. Orienting is about pulling your mental helicopter up when the idea seems unapproachable or too difficult and perspective is needed. It's also about coming closer to the ground so details are evident to explore more deeply and figure out the nuances. Each of the generalists we interviewed had their own search-specific ways of orienting themselves based on (1) what they already knew about the topic, (2) the range of resources available, and (3) their purpose (i.e., the importance of the search being undertaken).

Listen Carefully

Sonya, a student who suffered from migraines, wanted to research the topic of "cupping," a medical treatment that gained public attention when U.S. Olympic swimmers began using the practice. Her teacher, who had never heard of cupping, worried that the topic was too narrow to result in a good project. "What about researching alternative medicine in general?" she suggested. "Or maybe the science behind migraines?

Many teachers encourage students to make their topics bigger. For this teacher, who had never heard of cupping, the tendency was to ask Sonya to get oriented by starting with much more general questions. This was borne out of concern that Sonya would have trouble finding sources. But Sonya, whose Korean grandmother had introduced her to the practice of cupping, already knew a great deal about both cupping and migraines from personal experiences. Rather than investigate alternative medicine as a general topic—a search that would probably lead Sonya to do some superficial reading without answering her true curiosity—Sonya wanted to understand the science behind a process she had experienced personally. She needed to start closer to the ground, so to speak, and dig deeper.

What does orienting look like in practice? Here Joanna Cole, acclaimed author of the Magic School Bus series of books, offers a description of how she might go about writing a school report on leaves if she were a student.

> "First, here's what I wouldn't do," she tells us. "I wouldn't go to the encyclopedia as soon as I got to school and start copying down information. I wouldn't make an outline." Some people might do this, but not Joanna Cole. Instead, she would read in a "relaxed way." She would begin by looking for articles and books on trees and on plants and check to see if there was even a separate article on leaves. She would ask the librarian to help locate a few good books about plants with chapters on leaves and maybe they would even find a whole book about leaves.
>
> Then that evening she would spread all of that stuff out on her bed. She wouldn't worry about reading every word and she would try to keep an open mind. She would avoid picking out the first several facts and writing them down, one after another, without feeling a connection to her subject. She would want to see what information answered questions she always had; sometimes these were questions she didn't even know she had! Finally, the idea for the report would begin to take shape. (Cole and Saul 1996, 24)

For those of us who grew up finding information in printed text, understanding the concept of "reading around" or "reading in a relaxed way" or getting oriented is attached to processes we remember. While working in the library at a long wooden table stacked with books or sitting on the bed with books piled high, information was literally spread before us. To give contemporary learners—who tend to want their information needs answered quickly, via search engine—a sense of what this feels like, we recommend actually beginning with books and articles, with printed text. Going from one text to another actually slows down the process of finding information and helps dial down the mental speedometer. And the physicality of printed text offers students a visceral sense of what it feels like to browse. Our hope is that this experience can be transferred to the work they do on the Web.

For example, let's say that Marlene, the girl with the spider issue, was in your class. You might begin by bringing in a large pile of books to browse. Making a T-chart could be useful: on one side students list information that might help in thinking about the spider infestation (e.g., mating habits, diets) and on the other side interesting information that may not help with Marlene's problem (e.g., cool stuff about spiders to share with friends). You might even orchestrate a class discussion about what questions and facts students find most interesting. If students were to write a report inspired by this issue, what would they include? What else might they want to know? Once students have more knowledge about spiders and what interests them most, they might wish to do additional research, using sources they have at hand as well as new sources they find themselves.

It might be difficult at first to convince today's students that slowing down and looking around to get their bearings is a good thing and worth their time. However, we worry that when we only allow students to work with small, preselected text sets in an effort to be efficient with our time and support students' research, we prevent them from learning orienting behaviors that are critical to their success as generalist researchers.

"Let Us Be the Judge"

Carrie Launius, working with a class of fifth graders, invited students to nominate titles for a Science, Technology, Engineering, and Mathematics (STEM) book award. She began by reading aloud the award criteria identified by the National Science Teachers Association committee to her students and assuring them that finding award winners that met these criteria was a real problem with which librarians and adults were wrestling—in fact, she had helped create the award and was on the committee herself. Ms. Launius was clear in terms of the outcome she wanted, that students be able to explain the difference between the kind of thinking that goes into a STEM book and a straight science book, although she was also listening to the confusions they expressed so that she and the committee could revise as needed.

Ms. Launius's approach was to read aloud what she saw as clear examples of the categories—this one was surely a STEM book and this one was a science book. She did this as a read-aloud-think-aloud, modeling her thinking for the students as she read. When reading the science book, Ms. Launius noted interesting facts, diagrams, and content. But while reading the STEM book, she focused not just on the facts but rather on understanding what scientific and technological thinking and what activities were highlighted. She stopped to invite readers to think about the processes used by the featured characters (real or imaginary).

Next the students were invited to talk about how the two kinds of books were the same and different. Through this discussion, students were able to sort the books as STEM or non-STEM by applying the review criteria and considering how well the criteria applied. Finally, students were asked to examine the books that were piled around the room—recently published books as well as past winners. Students now had the materials as well as the conceptual understandings they needed to get oriented, and the conversations were robust.

Hunting for Multiple Perspectives

In a rural middle school, many students were involved in outdoor activities like hunting and fishing. When deer in the area were found to have chronic wasting disease, a highly contagious condition that has devastated deer populations in several states, students were interested in understanding more. They began their exploration by getting oriented to the situation using the state's department of conservation website. With their teacher's help, students created a list of questions about the disease and the controversial methods of controlling it and invited representatives from the conservation department's outreach division to speak at the class. They also divided into smaller groups and explored the issue from the perspective of hunters, landowners who profit from the hunting industry, and animal welfare advocates.

SOURCING

Although orienting has to do with what information you might choose to hunt for, sourcing has to do with where and how to find it. Expert generalists know a lot about the different kinds of sources that exist (government websites, types of books, newspapers, archives, peer-reviewed academic research, expert and stakeholder interviews, etc.) and when it's useful to access each.

The people who design search engines understand the almost invisible bridge between orienting and sourcing. They build algorithms to cross that bridge for us. And admittedly, they are pretty good at it. We type *getting rid of spiders* into a search box, and suggestions and alternatives—easily accessed by a single click—appear: "How to Get Rid of Spiders Naturally," "Spiders at the Lake House," "What Attracts Spiders to the House?" "Why do I Have Spiders in My House?" Lots of colorful advertisements for spider repellants are also presented. It is so easy and tempting to go with Google's suggestions, yet expert generalists know not to. They understand that Google—or whatever company has created the platform and algorithms—is run by people (with the flaws we all have) and exists to make a profit. Google is *not* an infallible, superhuman, altruistic librarian, out to spread truth.

Teacher Rob Lamb developed a strategy to demonstrate the kind of thinking he uses when sourcing information on the Web: the search-aloud-think-aloud (SATA).

The Search-Aloud-Think-Aloud

We credit Rob Lamb as the teacher who pioneered the SATA nearly ten years ago. Mr. Lamb learned about the read-aloud-think-aloud at one of Wendy's professional development workshops and regularly reads to his students from online sources. He described the day he decided to jump off the page he was reading and start searching for more information:

> I was trying to show students what it looks like to be a skeptical reader, and I found a piece about biodegradable, corn-based water bottles. As I was reading the article to the students, I realized this idea may be total crap. So, I started following the bread crumbs.

> We ended up clicking a lot of links and reading the fine print. Looking through the water bottle specs, we realized that the corn-based plastic, though completely organic, would probably melt on a July day in St. Louis: 90 degree temperature, 90 percent humidity, and 90 percent light. We also figured out that the bottle caps would not degrade at all. The caps had to be recycled separately. Then, in front of the class, I suddenly got the idea to see who funded this research. A few clicks later, and we realized that it was paid for by the Corn Council of America.

The SATA can be used to model "following the bread crumbs," or tracking information back to its source. It can also be used to demonstrate how readers can take advantage of the fact that the Internet is a "web" and information is connected. As Rob told us, "When I read an article, I don't read it as an isolated piece of information. I read it as connected to other pieces of information. My students were surprised by that. They've been taught for years to read from the beginning to the end, no matter what. But I don't do that, especially online."

FINDING A GUIDE

In addition to reading, expert generalists often turn to guides to help them navigate new terrain. What is the school equivalent of a guide? In some instances, it is you, the teacher. There may also be guides in the local community—your students' parents or instructors at the local community college or university. Librarians are great guides, and for K–12 students, college undergraduates might even make good guides. Consider institutional resources like museums, government agencies, or other nonprofits when reaching out for guidance—community outreach is often an expected part of their jobs. Think of guides as people who know the terrain, even if they don't know everything about the topic you (or your students) are pursuing.

Guides, in person or available through online communication, can introduce beginner generalists to ideas or references worth pursuing and may help identify relevant and knowledgeable contacts. A guide can also help novice researchers ask good questions or make decisions about credibility.

CONSOLIDATING AND SYNTHESIZING

The work of the generalist is an active, recursive process, not a linear one. Generalists mentally self-monitor as they move back and forth between orienting, sourcing, and consolidating/synthesizing information. At first their insights are tentative and wobbly. Insights are easy to discard when new information presents itself. As ideas solidify, we tend to become more attached to them. Generalists understand this tendency and mentally guard against it. As they investigate their questions, they build their understandings thoughtfully and deliberately, synthesizing and consolidating information from quality sources.

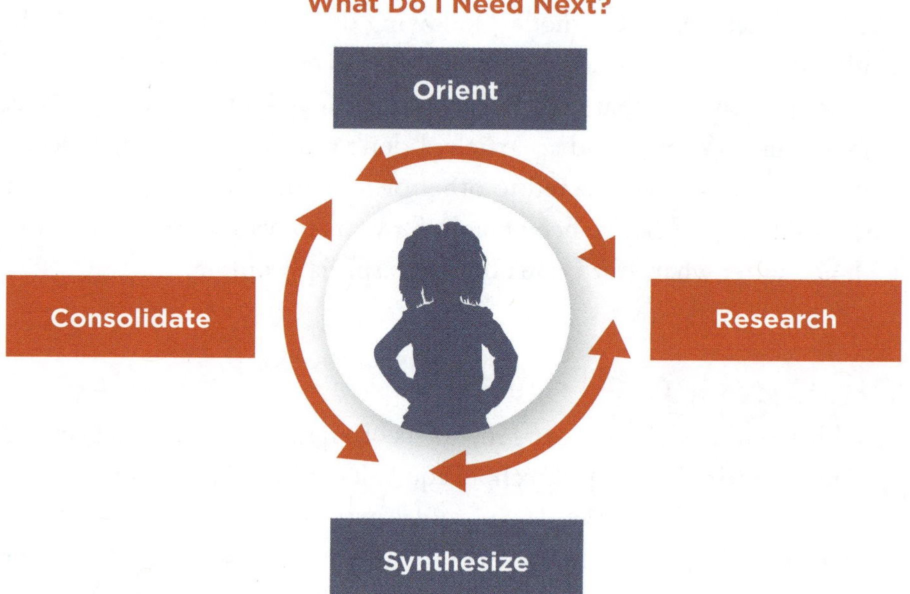

Figure 3.1

Though we consider synthesizing and consolidating together, they are not identical terms. Nor is consolidating a prerequisite for synthesizing. As they gather information, generalists are engaged in both processes in tandem. *Consolidating* is the act of gathering information and depends on basic comprehension skills. *Synthesizing* requires putting information together and seeing the connections and contradictions that emerge. It depends on higher-order thinking and critique.

Critical literacy scholar Hilary Janks (2018) points out that all texts (including movies, books, commercials, photographs, newspaper articles) invite readers to take up certain positions. A newspaper article about the California wildfires might invite you, the reader, to take up the position of well-informed yet skeptical individual, while an opinion article in the same newspaper on the same topic might invite you to take up the position of environmentally concerned citizen. And an action movie centered on firefighters battling a wildfire might invite you simply to relax and enjoy the special effects. (As readers engage with texts, Janks (2018) argues, they may take up one of two positions: the *ideal reader* or the *critical reader.*) Ideal readers are "ideal" from the perspective of the author of the text—they take up the positions offered with little resistance. We are all, at times, ideal readers, absorbing the information a text provided in exactly the manner the text's author might have wished. On the other hand, critical readers question the text, recognizing how they are being positioned and actively considering whether or not they wish to take it up. In the case of the opinion article about policies to contain California wildfires, ideal readers will accept the author's argument and, potentially, take action as a result. Critical readers will understand the author's argument but want to know more—they might look up additional information about wildfires and policies and put this information in conversation with the article. They might also recognize the techniques the opinion article writer is using to position them, especially if emotional language is used, and actively work to set aside their emotional reactions.

As generalists consolidate information, they may be acting more as ideal readers, metaphorically floating with the current and collecting information along the way. As generalists synthesize information, they put themselves into the critical reader framework, metaphorically paddling upstream. And, truth be told, every once in a while the generalist ends up in a whirlpool, not knowing if and how they wish to move along—with the current or against it.

Here is an example: a student athlete wants to improve his performance and read that titanium necklaces and bracelets might help him to do just that. The articles he found claim that the titanium stabilizes the electric flow that nerves use to communicate actions to the body and cited many sports stars who claim that the jewelry really helps. In this case the student was consolidating information, accepting the premise of the article and "going with the flow." But then, he began to think about how expensive one of these necklaces is, and he remembered that another kid on his team had one of the bracelets and he was having a terrible season. Then he began reading other articles, those written by scientists that offer a more skeptical perspective. Did he believe the skeptics who say that the titanium craze is junk science? He went back to the original articles and ads for the titanium jewelry, this time reading upstream.

Frankly, from a teaching perspective, it matters little what the student decided to do, but the process he engaged in was precisely what we would want to see happen from a generalist perspective. In synthesizing the information, the student was able to notice who he was as a reader at different times and the importance of stance in the acts of consolidating and synthesizing. We encourage readers and writers to monitor their own thinking as they gather work to consolidate and synthesize information. Many students seem to "feel" when they have lost their way, and they should trust that instinct, returning to the orientation or sourcing phase when they need to.

Synthesizing information or swimming upstream is surely more difficult than swimming downstream, that is, consolidating ideas and reading with the flow. We typically spend a lot of time in schools teaching consolidation. This work often goes under the name of "comprehension." But teaching synthesis is much harder. Naming these two processes, consolidating and synthesizing, is helpful. Differentiating and comparing the two are more helpful still. Offering students relevant examples is what often works best.

Synthesis should be seen as a creative act—looking for and finding the way information does or doesn't hang together. Lewis Mumford, the father of generalist thinking, came to what we are calling synthesis when standing on the Brooklyn Bridge and looking down at the vibrant and connected life below—the barges, the steamers being unloaded, the workers directing river traffic. Might this image be useful to young people trying to figure out what their teacher means by *synthesis*? Angela and Wendy have both stood on the banks of the Mississippi in St. Louis, looking at similar connections—the river traffic going north and south, the cars and trucks driving the highways and across the bridges, the trains, the planes, the people on foot headed toward the downtown or toward the Arch. How might this aerial perspective help students think about the ways they look for connections and contradictions in the information they encounter? What insights, what connections, might students make?

Generalists see from an aerial perspective, a more global perspective. Their synthesis is born from this perspective. They make inferences, and they think about purpose and relatedness. Information—whether talking about history, science, art, music, or the practical activities of child-rearing or caring for the infirm—is not viewed as static and isolated but rather in relation and connected. That feeling of making a connection, a connection that is supported by data, is a wonderful and memorable sensation. And even if the insights generated are not new to the world, there is a thrill in identifying something new from the aerial stance, something to check out further and discuss with others who have also stood on the bridge.

Interpretation Matters

Wendy recently attended a lecture on the history of one of the Scandinavian countries. The presenter began in about 1100 AD and, for ninety minutes, identified dates, rulers, and wars, finishing up with the European Union. Although the talk was well researched and correctly covered a lot of information, Wendy had no intellectual hooks on which to hang the information—and the speaker made no connections between the discreet items presented. Wendy left the talk puzzled and, within a few hours, forgot virtually everything she heard, except that it was a long history—in more ways than one.

Students regularly produce similar accounts—chronological lists of information that result in unsynthesized reports. For example, each student picks a body organ (one takes small intestine, another does liver, and another has the large intestine), and, using good sources, they might be able to tell you where the organ is located, what it is there to do, and what it looks like. But, without synthesis, students have simply acquired a lot of facts (probably pulled off a website verbatim). It's true, students did do some work by finding a site that describes the organ and drawing a picture of it. Yet, with a little more work on the part of the students and teacher, these reports could turn into a collaborative synthesis project. For example, students could be invited to understand the relationship between the organs working within a body system or to compare these organs in humans with their counterparts in other animals. *Synthesis* is ultimately an act of interpretation, born from an understanding of relationships or realized through comparison.

ORIENTING, SOURCING, AND SYNTHESIZING IN THE CLASSROOM: TWO STUDENTS ON AN INFORMATION-SEEKING QUEST

Imagine this: two eighth graders are both interested in the topic of diabetes. Lynda was diagnosed with type 1 diabetes at age six and has been living with the condition ever since. Gamal just heard that his grandmother was diagnosed with type 2 diabetes, and he wonders what this means for her health. When their teacher assigns the class a research presentation on a health-related topic, both Lynda and Gamal tell the teacher they want to research diabetes, and the teacher approves.

Getting Oriented

"Getting oriented" means getting the lay of the land before digging in deeply. Diabetes is a big topic—if Gamal and Lynda don't do some general reading on the subject first (or if they only make a half-hearted, cursory search), they'll produce simplistic, perhaps identical, and potentially plagiarized presentations. They also won't learn much about searching for information.

But Gamal and Lynda will get oriented from different places. Because Lynda has diabetes, she's familiar with terms like *insulin*, *blood sugar*, and *pancreas*. She also has a rudimentary understanding of the biology behind the condition. Perhaps most importantly, Lynda already has some go-to resources about diabetes—a children's book her parents gave her when she was first diagnosed (which also has a resource list at the end), her doctor (and she has an upcoming appointment), and the name of a reputable association (the American Diabetes Association) that she knows from the yearly fundraising walk her whole family participants in. She also happens to know that her cross-country coach has type 1 diabetes, too. Her teacher encourages her to get oriented by accessing these resources and using them to find others. Once she's explored for a bit, her teacher says, she can focus on a more specific question or topic.

On the other hand, Gamal knows almost nothing about diabetes—and he's a little scared for his grandmother's health. However, his teacher has encouraged him to spend some time getting oriented to his subject first by doing some general reading.

She encourages him to use online encyclopedias (including Wikipedia) to get an overview of the topic and find possible sources of information. Because Gamal is so new to this topic and Wikipedia entries can be difficult reading, she encourages him to use a kid-friendly search engine like kiddle.co to find background reading, too. She also directs him to three websites for general information on health conditions: WebMD.com, MayoClinic.org, and Kidshealth.org. She explains that WebMD includes peer-reviewed information, or information that at least one expert has checked for accuracy; that MayoClinic.org is a website run by one of the leading medical research hospitals in the country; and that kidshealth.org is a website run by a children's health system and written in language that's easy for kids to understand. All three websites are good for getting oriented to new health topics, she says. Gamal also may need to access some more general print resources, including the classroom's health textbook, for basic information about the endocrine system.

Both Lynda and Gamal spend some time reading widely about diabetes, looking for a basic understanding and additional questions or curiosities. They take some notes along the way, but they don't worry about writing down everything they learn because they are just getting a feel for their topics now, not researching for their presentations. After some time getting oriented, they return to their teacher to talk about their next steps.

After reading and talking with her doctor, her coach, her parents, and her small group in class (which includes Gamal), Lynda has a more focused topic. She's specifically interested in competitive athletes and type 1 diabetes. Her coach ran cross-country in college, and she knows some professional athletes have had diabetes. Her questions include both the science (How does exercise relate to the body's ability to regulate blood sugar?) and the human interest (What are the hardest things about dealing with diabetes as a competitive athlete? Have any really scary things ever happened to competitive athletes with type 1 diabetes?). She also wonders if there are particular sports that are dangerous for people with type 1 diabetes or if there would ever be a situation in which a person with type 1 diabetes would be encouraged *not* to participate in sports. Her teacher thinks this sounds like a great topic, and Lynda is off to work on a more focused search.

Now that Gamal thinks he understands the basics of his grandmother's diagnosis, he wants to know how he can help her live a healthy life. He recently overheard his grandmother tell his mother that she doesn't want to try too hard to regulate her blood sugar with diet and exercise because it would be easier to just take a pill. Gamal wonders about this. Should his grandmother try to control her diabetes without medicine? Would this mean she's cured? Are there advantages to taking medicine? What are the side effects? His teacher helps Gamal see that his topic is really about treatment options for type 2 diabetes, along with the pros and cons of each. She knows that there is the potential Gamal could answer his questions by simply going to one website and copying down all the information, so she also encourages him to think about what perspectives he might like to include. Does he want to talk with his grandmother? Perhaps with someone else who has diabetes (the teacher happens to know a few friends who have the condition whom she is sure would respond to an email from Gamal)? Perhaps he wants to write down some questions for his grandmother to bring to her next doctor's visit. She brainstorms with him for a few minutes, drawing upon what he's already read while getting oriented, before sending him off to do more research.

Sourcing

We use the term *sourcing* to refer to an understanding of where and how to find information related to a targeted information-seeking need. As Lynda and Gamal move from getting oriented into sourcing, they'll need to access multiple, credible sources of information—online, but also potentially in books or in the form of real people. Sourcing requires a basic understanding of what information can be found where: What kinds of questions and topics are best understood by reading books? Newspapers? Academic research? Blogs? Magazine articles? Encyclopedias? YouTube videos? (All of these may be accessed online.) Sourcing requires knowledge of the landscape of information: How does that information move from discovery onto websites or into newspapers?

Gamal and Lynda are both off to a good start—they've accessed several credible sources of information during their initial reading, and they've noticed that many of their first sources included links to other sources, too. Their teacher has explained to them that linked sources can be great additional resources when you're sure the original resource was a good one. (She's also cautioned that it doesn't work the other way—when you come upon a source you're not sure about, the fact that it links back to a credible source doesn't tell you anything about the new source's credibility. In fact, lots of suspicious sources link to credible ones to improve their *appearance* of credibility.) Both Lynda and Gamal go back to some of the sources they've already accessed, this time looking more carefully for specific kinds of information and links. This time, they keep track as they go of what they're learning, from where.

They both also have real people they can talk to, which makes their projects even more interesting. Their teacher encourages them to access real people when they can (see Chapter 7 for information on how to prepare students for interviews), especially when they have a personal connection. Gamal and Lynda work together to brainstorm interview questions and discuss whether some of their experts may be able to answer questions for both of them.

Finally, they each also start a few new searches. Lynda wants to put together a list of famous athletes who had type 1 diabetes as part of her presentation, and so she spends some time searching. She quickly realizes that just typing this question into a search engine leads to all different kinds of sources, none of which she's heard of before, so she goes to a Wikipedia page where there are hyperlinked references for each athlete listed. She knows she can double-check the information by clicking on the reference. As Gamal does more reading about diabetes, he continues to generate more questions: What does it mean that diabetes is progressive? What is the best eating plan for people with diabetes? Can you reverse diabetes? Gamal ends up on a lot of different websites with different answers to these questions, including websites that claim the government is hiding a diabetes cure to benefit the pharmaceutical industry. Gamal is suspicious of this site—which appears to contradict a lot of what he's already read—and shows it to his teacher. She praises him for his skepticism and for wanting to corroborate information across sources, and together they think about why this source may or may not be credible.

Consolidating and Synthesizing

Expert generalists don't wait until a search is finished to synthesize their information—they must consolidate, compare sources or corroborate information, monitor their own comprehension, and tentatively synthesize along the way. As Gamal and Lynda continue to gather information, their teacher builds in moments where they are forced to stop and take stock of their progress.

- Have they answered their original questions? If so, how do they know their answers are good ones?
- Have they found any information that seems contradictory?
- What should they do when two sources seem to disagree?
- Have their searches caused them to ask even more questions? If so, how important is it to answer these new questions?
- If their new questions are really important, do they need to do more orienting, or do they already know enough to keep going?
- Which of their sources are challenging to read? What are they doing when they are having trouble comprehending their sources?

Because Lynda and Gamal each have a personal interest in their topics, the process of synthesis is made somewhat easier. They aren't writing a diabetes report, gathering up the first ten facts they find online and putting them together in PowerPoint slides. Instead, they are looking for answers to authentic questions, questions that require them to seek information from a range of sources. As Lynda thinks about what her track coach said about exercise and diabetes, she naturally compares it to what she read in an online newspaper article about challenges of playing sports professionally with diabetes, and she puts this information in conversation with her understanding of the medical condition itself.

Lynda and Gamal also know they need to present their information to the class as part of a research roundtable day. Their teacher has told them they don't need to answer all their questions in this investigation—their presentations are supposed to end with a list of questions for future research—so Lynda and Gamal don't feel rushed to draw big conclusions about topics that are really hard to understand. As the research roundtable day approaches, Lynda and Gamal prepare their short talks, confident in their information and excited to share with their classmates.

What Did Lynda and Gamal Learn?

As Lynda and Gamal worked on their diabetes project, their teacher deliberately designed scaffolds to help them to engage with expert generalists ways of *doing*—orienting, sourcing, and synthesizing. They were also encouraged to learn a bit about their topics before focusing on a specific question or issue (to *explore* before they *investigate*). They were encouraged to tap into their existing background knowledge as part of the orienting process. When they were ready to narrow their topics, their teacher helped them identify an area of focus that tapped into their true curiosity, while also being small enough to be investigated in the time allotted. Once the targeted searching began, their teacher helped them think in context-specific ways about what constitutes a good source of information and why. Rather than relying on an arbitrary checklist or a list of rules about sources, their teacher supplied them with some initial sources and explained why these were good. As the students continued looking, the teacher helped them think about their sources and praised them when they asked questions or showed signs of skepticism. Finally, the students didn't need to finish their topics by the end of the project—they were encouraged to list additional questions and to present just what they had learned so far.

Through this activity, the students were able to learn a generalist way of *knowing*: the ability to learn about something new or unfamiliar. This involved also learning about how information moves into the world. When Gamal landed on a suspicious website, his teacher helped him think about how that website came to be online—and why. She taught the whole class about the information cycle (see Illinois Library n.d.), or the process by which information moves from its origins (in the form of an event or a discovery) and into books, magazines, newspapers, or the Internet. When possible, she encouraged the students to get back to the original source of information, as Lynda did when she clicked the Wikipedia hyperlinks to find newspaper articles about athletes with type 1 diabetes. When Lynda found an article in which an athlete was quoted talking about her diabetes, Lynda knew she had accessed what's known as "original reporting."

Finally, the project helped students develop generalist *ways of being*: curious, open-mindedly skeptical, and persistent. As Gamal and Lynda ran into dead ends on their searches, their teacher demonstrated how to try new search terms or to brainstorm other possible sources, modeling persistence. Gamal and Lynda also worked in a small group throughout the project and were encouraged to share their most fascinating pieces of information with their group at the beginning of each class. To do so, they took what one author we interviewed called "oh wow notes," or notes on information that amazed them. These moments of sharing fostered curiosity among the class in all kinds of topics. Finally, because they were sharing this information publically with one another and because they were personally invested in what they found, both Gamal and Lynda cultivated a sense of open-minded skepticism. They wanted to find accurate information, and they needed to be willing to learn something that might change their minds.

Deborah's "Oh Wow!" Notes

We borrowed the idea of oh wow notes from award-winning nonfiction author Deborah Heligman who described her research process to us this way:

> I only note the things that make me say, "Oh wow" or "Ew gross," or "I can't believe it!" I call these my "oh wow notes." When I am ready to write, I look over my notes, and then *put them away.* I write my first draft from memory—because I know the things I remember will be the things I want to impart to my readers. These are those things that will make them say, "Oh wow!" when *they* read my books. I can always go back to look up the infrastructure that will hold up my oh wows (dates, numbers, other less memorable facts). That's my process, and it seems to me that's what being a generalist and a writer has taught me.

NOW IT'S YOUR TURN!

The very best way to help your students understand information orienting, sourcing, and consolidation—and the relationship of information finding to the personal characteristics of curiosity, open-minded skepticism, and persistence—is to show your students how such characteristics work for you. For that reason, we devote Part II of this book to helping you to work through an information search of your own. By sharing your own experiences and decision making with students, you provide an authentic example of the generalist's approach to dealing with information curiosities and needs.

Part II

A SELF-GUIDED COURSE

Our tendency as teachers (and teacher educators) is to immerse ourselves in the practices we eventually wish to teach, to understand a new concept or skill from the perspective of a learner before translating that concept or practice for our students. In Part II, we invite you into a self-guided course where you will develop your own generalist literacy identity. In the chapters that follow, you will be encouraged to identify and investigate a topic and to reflect on the moves you make as you do so. Throughout this section we've also supplied classroom application ideas and glimpses into the classrooms of real teachers working in classrooms across the country.

Chapter 4

GETTING STARTED

Every informational quest begins somewhere. In this chapter, we'll start down the generalist path by locating possible topics from real life. Finding a good topic to explore is an important step in this self-guided course and for classroom teachers—but remember that the topic itself is less important than the *informational search process* the topic inspires. Generalists are essentially experts at *how to learn from sources*—what you choose to learn as you make your way through this section will be secondary to the process you experience. That said, a great topic can carry you along when you are frustrated or run into dead ends. Because you really want to know more, or need to know more, it may motivate you when you run into problems. This is even more important for your students who may need support in developing the persistence necessary to wade through an abundance of information or to start over when information is scarce.

Luckily, good topics are all around us. We'll start with an example from Angela's life: a few years ago, Angela, her husband, and her daughters (aged seven and four) moved from Missouri to Florida. As lifelong Midwesterners, they were not completely prepared for the new environment. Over the course of the summer, as they got acclimated and attempted to get ready for the new school year, their lives were filled with informational needs. Here are just a few of their questions from the month of July alone:

- How do you establish state residency in Florida? How soon do we need to do that to enroll our daughters in school?
- What school are we zoned for? What's it like?
- What are the health requirements for starting public school? How do we get the correct forms so our daughters can start on time? How do we get a doctor to evaluate our children when we still have Missouri health insurance that isn't accepted at a lot of places?
- What is going on with the lizards living in the mailbox? Why do some have bright red throats that expand like bubble gum bubbles?
- Why is it that wherever we move there is one cable company monopoly and they always have terrible customer service?
- Is all this rain common or unusual?
- Why does everyone here park in the grass? Why doesn't it tear up the ground?
- Why is our water bill so high?
- What kind of bird makes that noise at night?
- Is Spanish moss really moss?
- What tips do we need for alligator safety?

- Why is there no food for sale at the farmer's market? What is the growing season here?
- Why does it seem so much darker here than anywhere we've ever lived?
- Where is Silver Glen Springs? Is it okay that the summer camp wants to take the kids there on a bus tomorrow?
- Why is food so much more expensive here than what we're used to?
- Why are we being advised to prepare for hurricane season when we are miles from the coast?
- We promised the girls a puppy when we moved—what kind of dog will be right for our family?

The list could go on forever, but let's stop there.

As you can see, Angela's family's questions were inspired by a variety of things. Some were straightforward "need to know" kinds of questions. They *needed* to know how to get state residency to move forward on a lot of things. They *needed* to find the Department of Motor Vehicles, the closest bank, a new doctor, and dentist.

Other questions were inspired by curiosity. Their new home was a mystery, a brand-new world. The ecosystem was radically different from what they were used to. There were few hills and less variability in the weather, and cold-blooded animals were everywhere. Customs were also a mystery they wanted to understand. Street names (or numbers), the way people dressed, the patterns of life in a college town during the summer, cuts of meat that were and were not available at the meat counter in the grocery store—these were things they were curious about, though they didn't *need* to know the answers in the same way they needed to know what day school started.

When you move to a new place, there are also all kinds of questions that hover in between the zones of curiosity and need. They weren't sure if they *needed* to understand alligators to go tubing down the Ichetucknee River or if alligator safety was something they were simply curious about (or, in the case of Angela's husband, obsessed with). Every day as they went about their lives, read the paper, watched the local news, and talked to neighbors, they were presented with new questions, new curiosities, new controversies, new needs.

Some they answered. Some they let go. Some started them down a path of cascading questions and information seeking that continues to this day. Some were straightforward and answered with a quick Google search.

All of the questions were invitations to explore nonfiction texts. Many of them were perfect invitations to write nonfiction, too. We (Angela and Wendy) both love teaching nonfiction reading and writing because we are curious people. And the best teachers we know are curious too. As you move through this section of the book, take the opportunity to indulge in your own wonder, awe, and desire to learn.

Finding a Topic

Now that Angela has shared a list of questions from her life, start generating a list of your own. Try this: set a timer for seven minutes and find a place to write (either a blank Word document or a notebook). For seven minutes, write as many questions (or general topics of interest) as you can think of. Don't censor yourself—no question is too big or too small for this activity. Follow your brain wherever it wants to go. When your timer goes off, stop and read over what you have, add or delete a few ideas if necessary, and save your document for later.

Over the past several years, Angela has taught a course on nonfiction reading and writing to preservice and inservice teachers. Hundreds of students have completed the previous brainstorming activity and generated many, many questions, ranging from How do you become a Rockette? to What organizations in Florida help abandoned golden retrievers? to Why am I always sick at the beginning of the school year?

The best questions tend to be ones that the seeker is genuinely fascinated by, that connect somehow to the seeker's individual identity or innate curiosity. The teachers with whom Angela works also report enjoying the exercise of asking questions and, ultimately, exploring issues. They comment that they don't often pursue their own curiosities in systematic and thoughtful ways, even though they may spend a lot of time online or being bombarded with incidental information. The idea that one can thoughtfully explore curiosities and answer questions is the key to her course and to this book.

After working with lots of teachers and students on informational investigations, we've found that some of the greatest topics come when the following conditions are present:

- The researcher/writer is personally interested in the topic.
- Information is readily available on the topic.
- The topic is not completely "settled"—there's something "new" going on.
- The topic connects to the curriculum in some way.

We call this the "sweet spot"—the student has personal investment in the project, the information isn't too challenging to find (obstacles can lead to persistence, but too many challenges can just lead to frustration), the topic is timely (therefore people are talking about it and potentially experts have opinions on it), and the student and teacher have the right background knowledge to make sense of the information because it connects back to the curriculum.

The final point—the curriculum—may be the least important of the three. We've seen students engage in great investigations that are only tangentially related to traditional school curriculum. However, when the topic connects to what the students are learning in school, the projects may be even more powerful (and easier to justify as a teacher).

"I Don't Have Any Questions!"

We both love the question-generating activity, but some of our teacher friends prefer a different approach. Instead of brainstorming questions to begin a new project, they look for topics in the world and try to find ones that connect to the curriculum. We also encourage you to revisit your activities from Chapter 1—incidental and intentional information, importance, and preparation—to see if any topics are lingering there. Finally, we are reminded of a question science journalist Alan Newman always asked students who were trying to identify topics for a science news story: "What do you like to do outside of school?" Whether the answer is "sleep," "exercise," "play video games," or "volunteer at the local animal shelter," a curiosity or question could usually be found lurking nearby. The student interested in playing video games investigated the "red ring of death" plaguing Xbox 360 video game consoles at the time; the student who liked exercise investigated a local running club and the research on the benefits and drawbacks of exercising in groups.

If you can't find a topic, try Dr. Newman's suggestion. Brainstorm focused questions related to a hobby or freewrite about a broad area of interest. What are you curious about? What has been in the news lately? What have you always wanted to understand but never taken the time to look into?

Questions and curiosities that arise from real life are a great way to begin an intentional information-seeking project. But what do you do next? As you probably noticed from Angela's list, not all questions are created equal. Our next step, then, is to think about the different kinds of questions that life inspires—and the different possibilities for teaching that each offers.

Although questions can be categorized in a lot of different ways, for our purposes, let's think about questions according to two different criteria:

1. Needs versus wants (and the ground in between)
2. Complexity

A single question can be categorized by both variables, and one variable doesn't predict any of the others (i.e., all needs are not complex).

IS IT A NEED OR A WANT?

Need-to-Know Questions

We consider questions "need to know" if they require an answer for the questioner to move forward in life. Rather than getting into a philosophical discussion of needs versus wants, we'll assume you can be the judge of whether a question represents a need. And one person's want may be another's need.

Some need questions are quite simple to answer. Remember your first few days of college. When you arrived on campus, you probably had a lot of need questions that involved no more than a Google search or a search of the university website, questions like How do I get to my first class from my residence hall (or parking lot)? or Where do I get a student ID?

However, need questions are not always simple or straightforward. Remember your first job offer (or imagine it!). You needed to answer a basic question: Should you accept the job? Questions about employment are urgent, have deadlines, and are really important to your life (and the lives of those who love you). But answering the question involves a lot more than googling *Should I accept the job?* or even *What's it like to work at this school?* You probably looked into the community where the job was located (maybe researching cost of living, weather, local amenities, etc.), the curriculum that you might be expected to teach, the school or school district's rating. You may have talked to other people who work there. You might have investigated salary, salary schedule, or job benefits. If the job involved a move and you had a partner's career to consider, your search may have been even more complicated. If you decided to accept the position, your questions probably didn't stop there. Now you were filling out paperwork and making decisions about things like how many deductions to claim for tax purposes, perhaps, or the best retirement savings plan. You were also planning for your first days of teaching—and answering questions like how to arrange your classroom and which activities to do for the first day of school. Whew!

Want-to-Know Questions: Our Curiosities

On the other hand, you probably have a lot of questions that are inspired by curiosity, those you can live without answering but that nag at you, that make you into a curious, engaged human being. Questions inspired by curiosity can be simple or complex—for Angela, learning more about the lizards in her yard was fairly simple, but understanding hurricanes and their impact was more complicated. Want-to-know questions can also be divided into those that come from a "helicopter view" of life and those that come from being "on the ground." For example, as the 2016 election neared, Angela's older daughter asked her where the Obama family would live once the new president moved into the White House. "Does somebody tell them where to go, or do they get to pick?" This was certainly not a question that emerged directly from her life but, instead, one that came from a helicopter view of the presidency and a curiosity inspired by her class's study of the branches of government. In schools, the curriculum can be an inspiration for these kinds of helicopter view questions; for us, as adults, our NPR station and other sources of news inspire many of our helicopter curiosities. On the other hand, Angela's younger daughter regularly has her curiosity piqued by the various insects and other creatures she encounters from being on the ground (literally and figuratively!) in Florida.

The word *curious* sometimes connotes playfulness. However, just because we contrast curiosity with need doesn't mean we think that our want-to-know questions are inherently less valuable than our need-to-know ones. In fact, being curious—or, as Merriam-Webster defines it, being "marked by a desire to investigate and learn"—can lead to some of our most important learning. Over the past five years, as we have worked with countless teachers and students on the ideas that grew into this book, we have been inspired by curiosity to learn more about topics such as the Syrian refugee crisis; water in Flint, Michigan; and immigration policy. Even though for us these topics didn't have a direct impact on our lives (we could have gone through our days without knowing anything about them at all), we felt it was important to understand them. And we suspect no one would consider these topics frivolous or unserious.

The Space in the Middle

Of course, some questions fall in between needs and wants. In fact, sometimes you are asking a question to *determine* whether you have a need or a want. For example, when the Zika virus first appeared in the news, many people were curious about it. For us, curiosity was inspired by empathy for the afflicted and by wonder that this disease appeared to come from nowhere. For Angela and her family in Florida, the question was a little more pertinent than for Wendy, who was living in Missouri at the time. Angela had questions, read information, and thought about the virus and its relationship to her family and health, in part to determine whether understanding Zika was a need or a want (for Angela's colleague who was pregnant at the time, the information-seeking process was even more urgent—real-world information seeking always connects to your personal circumstances). Our questions may move us back and forth between needs and wants, too. A question that starts as a need to know (e.g., What is my daughter's zoned school like?) may lead us to ask other questions (e.g., Why are all the magnet programs located in certain parts of town?).

WHAT KIND OF INFORMATION AM I SEEKING?

We can also categorize our questions based on the kinds of answers we think we'll find—and the complexity and/or certainty of those answers. Of course, we don't always know how complicated our questions are when we ask them—as we get into researching, we may discover a seemingly simple topic is quite nuanced while a topic we thought was complicated is really straightforward—but the level of complexity is a big factor in how we search for information.

Understanding a question's complexity is connected to the generalist skill of *sourcing*. Expert generalists know where to go for information and *why they might want to check more than one source.* Generalists know that some questions can be answered by going directly to the original source of information, and others require a lot more orienting and, later, digging. In schools, we sometimes arbitrarily assign a number of sources for a research project, but in real life figuring out why you might look at multiple sources—and which sources you should consult—is much more complex.

Do I need more than one source? **It depends on the question!**

Information Sought	Example	Why Might You Look at More Than One Source?
Single data point or fact, unlikely to be incorrect	Distance between two cities	Verification (Note: for some single data point questions, generalists don't need to go to more than one source. Instead, they go straight to the *original source*, the place where information is generated. For example, if you wanted to know a population number in the United States, the Census Bureau is mandated to produce that figure.)
Single data point or fact, controversial (i.e., measured differently by different organizations, disputed, controversially defined)	Adult literacy rate in the United States	Verification, looking for consensus, understanding the various ways the information is generated, a key term is defined, or a construct is measured
Entertainment	Pop culture news, current events, "idle" questions	Background information, following a trail backward or to tangentially related topics
Opinion or recommendation (consumer or non-life-threatening/changing)	Best treatment for child's ear infection; best new software for home music recording	Consensus, desire to feel confident in decision
Information to understand a complex topic	Food pricing in different parts of the country	Understanding different perspectives; different parts of the complex topic explained in different resources; verification and consensus of information
Opinion or recommendation (life-threatening/changing)	Impact of upcoming legislation on our community; best treatment for cancer	Need to understand an issue from multiple perspectives; desire to look at expert and stakeholder perspectives

Figure 4.1

The Best Topics are Your Own Topics

Return to the list of questions you generated earlier in this chapter. If necessary, spend a few minutes adding some more. You may also want to review your notes on incidental/intentional sources of information (Chapter 1). Once you have a good list of questions or topic ideas, spend some time rereading them. Are some grouped around a similar topic? Is there a "big" question lingering somewhere, with a lot of smaller questions nested inside? Which questions are inspired by curiosity? Which by a real need to know? Which are complex? Think about your questions in terms of the importance/preparation graphic in Figure 1.2—what kind of question or topic do you want to explore?

Your eventual goal is to identify something you'd like to spend time investigating as you move through the rest of this book. You want a just-right topic—not so big you'd be better off writing a book, not so small you can answer it with a quick Google search. It will be something that you feel driven to explore (driven by curiosity or need, that's up to you). If you want to share your process in your own classroom, choose a topic that's something suitable for and of interest to students. Your topic needs to be something you can find sources of information on—not something you know everything about already, but not something that is either so new there's no information available (i.e., a science breakthrough that was announced yesterday) or something that is simply unanswerable with sources (i.e., What happens when we die?).

At this point you may have a very general topic, a few possible topics, or a group of related questions that may turn into a topic—remember, your topic will evolve once you begin *orienting* yourself to it. Don't worry if this whole process scares you or if you're not sure what makes a topic good—this is messy, nonlinear work. You can't get it wrong, and you do get better with practice.

When you're ready, engage in some more writing about your topic. Set a timer (ten minutes is a good amount of time) and start writing, promising yourself you won't stop until the timer goes off. Write about your topic, the questions that inspired you, the things you hope to learn, the questions you have. If you have a writing group, you may also turn this activity into "oral brainstorming"—answer the same questions out loud with a friend. Five minutes of talking it out—without interruption—is usually adequate.

QUESTIONS, COMPLEXITY, AND THE CLASSROOM

We introduced complexity as a variable to consider because different kinds of questions allow you to do different things in the classroom. If you (or a student) has a need-to-know question that calls for a single, uncontested data point to answer, you can model your generalist skills by doing a search-aloud in front of the class (i.e., go to your favorite search engine or directly to the known source and find the answer, verbalizing your thinking along the way). Likewise, questions that call for a single but contested answer allow you to model what happens when you compare answers across sources of information. In both cases, the search-aloud is also a way to demonstrate that even teachers don't know everything—and to create a classroom where questioning and information seeking are part of the climate.

Questions that call for a single data point usually don't lead to great topics for extended information searches. Other questions may be complex but simply not important enough to pursue. A good topic resonates with you as a human being—all good topics come round to the self.

"Huh?" A Teacher Steps Aside

"Who has a good idea for a topic to investigate?" the teacher asked her eighth-grade students. We were working with a middle school science teacher to bring authentic reading and writing to her classroom. All three of us—Wendy, Angela, and the classroom teacher—were surprised with Cody's answer: "I want to understand how instant cameras work."

"Instant cameras?" the teacher asked, trying to hide her skepticism. This was years before the instant camera comeback was in full swing, and, to our much older ears, the topic didn't sound like a promising way for a student to access and assess current sources. "What makes instant cameras interesting to you?"

"Lady Gaga," the student replied (we could almost hear his unspoken *duh*). Many other students nodded. In fact, they looked at us like we were crazy for not knowing that Lady Gaga had an endorsement deal with Polaroid and used instant cameras in her music videos.

The teacher wisely decided to get out of the way. "Wow! I didn't know that. Sounds like a great topic. Let me know what you find out." One of the great joys of teaching is helping students connect with topics and ideas that they may never encounter otherwise. However, you may find that when you let your students choose their own topics, *you* learn something new, too. There's no better way to model curiosity than to let your students see you truly fascinated by something they've discovered.

Scaffolded Searches

When you send students out to do intentional information seeking, it doesn't always need to be an individual project. The first investigation of the school year, for example, might be something the whole class works on. Perhaps inspired by a read-aloud, the curriculum, or an interest of the teacher, students can all investigate an aspect of a whole-class question or topic. To read more about one class's first investigation of the year, see Chapter 10. The teacher may choose to model her own investigation alongside the students. For younger students, a single class-wide question may even be appropriate as a first step—the class does all the searching, reading, and talking together.

As students gain practice with this kind of investigating, you may consider putting them into teams for a project. After all, we live in a connected world. As adults, very rarely do we absolutely have to seek out and understand information all by ourselves—we may choose to do so as a matter of preference, but people are nearly always available to turn to if we get stuck or want to bounce ideas around. When Angela's family got a new puppy, she read obedience books and looked online for vet's offices—but she also talked to friends who have dogs.

Students in small groups function in the same way. When they are all interested in a particular question or topic, they can support one another. They can read different texts and compare what they find. They also bring in different kinds of background knowledge and perspectives on the question and can challenge one another or provide a different way of thinking.

At other times, you may find that students need a chance to do their own investigations. You may create a very broad category—everyone is looking into a history question, for example—but each student's topic will be his or her own. This takes a lot more work on the part of the teacher to be sure students have workable topics and find credible sources, but it also can result in the highest level of student engagement.

In all cases, keep the big goal in mind: students are learning *how to learn something new by engaging with credible sources, accessed online and in person.* They can do this alone, as a whole class, or in a small group—and, ideally, during the course of a school year they will have chances to do all three.

Chapter 5

GETTING ORIENTED

As teachers get started with this work, we have noticed two tendencies when it comes to helping students choose topics for information-seeking projects—we either push students to expand their ideas (to go too big) or rush students to focus on their topics before students are ready (narrow too soon). Both of these tendencies are understandable! Choosing a good topic is hard, and the curricular calendar often looms. However, as our expert generalists taught us, sometimes you need to take a little time to *orient yourself* to a new topic or field before you can do anything else. The process of getting oriented is often skipped in school research projects, but taking the time to explore in the beginning can ultimately save a lot of time down the road—and can make the research process much more valuable. So, how do you get oriented? In this chapter, we'll outline various ways to get the lay of the land when you're investigating a new topic.

Remember, however, even though we describe getting oriented as an early stage to a research project, intentional information seeking isn't linear. Sometimes you start with a highly specific question and realize that you actually need to do some background reading first. Other times you read broadly because you have only a general idea of what you want to learn and you need to know more before you can focus. And, on still other occasions, you go back and forth between general background reading and more targeted searches throughout the research process. As you engage in the process of getting oriented to your topic or question, notice the kinds of research and reading skills you need for this part of the process. These getting oriented skills will probably be slightly different from the research and reading skills you need when your searches are more focused.

BACKGROUND READING

As expert generalists know, general background reading can be an incredibly important first step (see Chapter 3 for more about orienting). The less you know about a topic, the more important your background reading is.

Imagine a photograph of a person or a place you love. When you know something or someone well, you can often recognize them, even when the camera is zoomed in incredibly close (even if you can only see the outline of the person's cheek or part of the building's roofline). However, if the photograph is of a historical figure you don't know well, or of a landmark in a foreign country, you may need the photographer to be further back, to include not only the person or building but also the surroundings (the Oval Office or the rest of the London skyline).

Think of background reading in the same way. If you have a question about a topic you know fairly well, you can probably start with more specific resources (or, to continue the metaphor, zoomed in close). When Angela investigates the local school her daughters may attend, she has a lot of background knowledge about educational policies, curriculum, and technical jargon that she can use to make sense of her reading. She can start getting oriented directly on the school district's website, perhaps, or by reading state educational policy documents that might be difficult for someone with less background knowledge.

How Much Do They Really Know?

A student proposed learning more about the advantages of electronic cigarettes over regular cigarettes, a topic the teacher knew very little about (but one that the student had firsthand experience with). Nervous that the topic might be controversial or difficult to research, the teacher hesitated. "What about researching the dangers of nicotine? Or how to quit smoking?" the teacher countered.

We understand the teacher's hesitation—and we know that teachers must use their judgment and knowledge of the local context when approving topics. When student-proposed topics aren't blatantly inappropriate or illegal, though, we encourage teachers to let student interest lead the way. Yet student interest can come with a second challenge: when students know a topic well (especially from firsthand experience), they may be less interested in investigating the topic with an openmind and more interested in "proving" their point of view (in this case, that electronic cigarettes were harmless).

Getting oriented when you know a topic well may mean you can start with a much more focused search and do your reading on more specialized websites than you might when you know very little about your subject. However, if a topic is very emotional for you (or your student), getting oriented may also mean finding a way to see a familiar topic with new eyes or from a different point of view.

On the other hand, when you know almost nothing about a topic, when you need to start your search from the panoramic camera angle, you probably have some go-to resources you use. What are they? When we ask young people this question, many answer, "Google." Young people tend to consider search engines—especially Google—a "source" for a few reasons. First, and most obviously, it's the place they go to find information—it's the source, in the same way the library might have been the source of knowledge in the pre-Internet days. Second, for some basic (usually uncontroversial) questions, Google supplies the "answer" in a box without any obvious link to other sources. It is the "source" of information about how to convert gallons to liters, for example, or which team won the big game last night. Google search pages didn't always look this way (and may look still different in the future), which illustrates the changing landscape of online information and the reason that we must focus our instruction on orientations and dispositions toward information rather than only on technical skills. Technology is constantly changing, and the skills of today may not be the skills needed in just a few years.

As an adult, you probably use a search engine to locate general or orienting information, too, but you are also more sophisticated in how you think about the results page. Stanford researchers coined the term *click restraint* to describe the way highly skilled information seekers scanned the list of search engine results to find a credible source, rather than clicking on the first thing that appeared. In contrast, they noted that many young people are "promiscuous clickers," clicking indiscriminately on the first several results until they got an answer, sometimes regardless of how credible that answer was (Wineburg and McGrew, 2019). If you are starting out to learn about a new topic, you may scan the list of search results and look for the following kinds of sources:

- An online encyclopedia such as Wikipedia (see "Wikipedia" information box one page 75) or, for students, a kid-friendly equivalent (See Chapter 2 for recommendations of such sites.)

- A highly credible news site (one with an editorial board, reporters who engage in original reporting, and a mechanism for publishing corrections when there are errors), such as the *New York Times* or the BBC (Note that, on many news sites, it is becoming difficult to tell editorial and opinion pieces from objective reporting and even *when* an article is objectively reported. When your information need is important, you should always consult more than one news source to see the different ways a topic is covered; see Figure 4.1.)

- A subject-specific general website such as WebMD or the Mayo Clinic (for health questions)

- A government organization that deals with your topic such as the U.S. Census Bureau, the Centers for Disease Control and Prevention, or the National Oceanographic and Atmospheric Organization

- A YouTube video from a credible organization or person

- A first-person perspective on your topic such as a blog, a discussion forum, or an op-ed piece (For many topics, you wouldn't want to look *only* at first-person perspectives, but they can be useful for stakeholder perspectives, or, sometimes, background or overview information.)

When getting oriented to a new topic, your goal is to get background information, to understand the broad picture, to do some general reading before you can get into more specific or technical research. At this stage, it is very important that you're getting credible information, but you don't need to stick to the kinds of information you would cite in an academic paper. Part of the process of getting oriented when researching the best puppy for your family to adopt might include reading some new puppy owner blogs—definitely not academic sources, but potentially worthwhile orienting information for this kind of topic nonetheless. Orienting information also often includes "tertiary" sources (or those sources that bring together information from primary and secondary sources and synthesize it in a way that's easy to understand, i.e., encyclopedias), resources you'd rarely cite in formal writing (see Chapter 7 for more on primary, secondary, and tertiary sources).

If your topic is more settled—less controversial, with less "new" information coming out—your best resources for orienting information may not be online at all. Don't forget the power of books or physical magazines that you may have at home or in the classroom. Students may also use the curriculum for background information—textbooks can provide concise overviews of a lot of topics that may inspire more specific research questions.

Getting Oriented When You Know Very Little

A narrow topic is usually better than a broad one, but it may be hard to narrow a topic before you know anything about it. For example, one student was really interested in the state of Florida. The teacher recognized that this was far too broad a topic and the following dialogue ensued:

Teacher: What about the state of Florida?

Student: What makes Florida unique, I've never lived anywhere else, and I'm curious what we have in Florida that they don't have other places.

Teacher: Do you mean plants? Animals? Businesses? Things to do?

Student: I'm not sure. All of it.

Teacher: How about this—why don't you do some reading for background and see what grabs your attention. For this project, you'll need to be a little narrower, but it sounds to me like you don't quite know what interests you the most right now. How about you read for a bit and let's talk again?

The teacher directed the student to a few books about the state and recommends two general state-focused websites, one on natural resources and one about tourism. After doing some initial investigating, the student came back excited to learn more about the threats to the ecosystem by invasive species. After another conversation with the teacher, the student went off to read more about Burmese pythons and what wildlife experts were doing to try to control the species. The teacher knew about the Burmese python problem prior to the first conversation with the student but would never have been able to guess that this particular issue in the state of Florida would grab the student's attention. The student had to do some reading on his own first.

We Like Wikipedia

When Wikipedia was first launched, the fact that anyone could edit the pages was alarming, and many schools blocked the site. Over time, though, Wikipedia's editorial process has evolved. Although many still claim "anyone can put anything on a Wikipedia page," it's actually not so easy.

Wikipedia pages are monitored, corrected frequently, and can be protected from editing, either because of coordinated attempts to sabotage information or because the content is settled (look for the icon of a lock next to the article title). Wikipedia even has levels of protection, including semi-protected (at the time of this writing, the entry for oxygen was semi-protected) and extended-confirmed protection (at the time of this writing, the entry for Donald Trump had this level of protection). Though the process of correcting information isn't perfect, Wikipedia's ability to rapidly update its content also makes it a *better* source in some ways than the print encyclopedias of old. If you'd like a behind-the-scenes look at the editorial process of Wikipedia, click the "talk" tab at the top of each entry (it is found next to the "article" tab). Here you can see information about why the article is protected (if applicable), along with questions and comments about the article's content.

Wikipedia has also attracted many contributors who are interested in ensuring the accuracy and currency of the information. The idea of a crowdsourced encyclopedia was revolutionary at the time of Wikipedia's launch in 2001, but Wikipedia has attracted thousands of contributors who add and edit content (Wikipedia claims two edits are made every second), many of them from highly qualified experts. We have heard of graduate students at MIT being allowed to contribute to Wikipedia pages about mathematical algorithms as part of their coursework, with their work checked by their professor. The participation of these experts has had a second effect—the content on Wikipedia has sometimes gotten more difficult to understand for a layperson, especially the science content.

Despite their efforts, Wikipedia will probably always contain some inaccuracies and deliberate hoaxes. In one instance, college students edited a page about the children's book series Amelia Bedelia and the falsehoods they inserted stayed on the page for five years, even making their way into other credible sources of information (see the "talk" page on the Amelia Bedelia entry for more on this). We've also heard stories of teachers *requiring* students to make false edits to Wikipedia, either to prove that Wikipedia is not a good source of information or to demonstrate how quickly content is corrected. We don't support these assignments. If you would like to help your students understand the credibility of Wikipedia content, engage in a search-aloud with them and demonstrate how to click the links and verify information outside the website.

Like print encyclopedias and textbooks, Wikipedia is not a primary or even a secondary source and is not appropriate to cite in academic research for the same reason encyclopedias weren't appropriate—they are simply too far from the original information. However, Wikipedia (and other encyclopedias) is *wonderful* for orienting information. Wikipedia articles can also be a good source of search terms for use in a search engine or database. For instance, *life on other planets* left a student with bogus stories about little green men, whereas, when he found and used the term *astrobiology* that he learned from Wikipedia, his search was definitely more successful. Wikipedia articles also link to primary and secondary sources (look at the bottom of the page) that *can* be used in more formal research. In this way, Wikipedia can be better than some textbooks that don't cite any sources.

Logging Your Journey

Look at the brainstorming you completed at the end of the Chapter 4. How much do you already know about your topic? What kind of orienting information will help you move forward?

If you are pursuing a topic that you are already familiar with or that has clear go-to websites for orienting information, you might begin your initial search for information on a specialized website. For example, if you are interested in Mars exploration, you may start at NASA.gov or the BBC's space coverage (BBC.com/earth/tags/space). If your question is related to international travel, you may explore the Central Intelligence Agency's World Factbook. On the other hand, if you know nothing about your topic or there are no clear websites for background information, you may decide to start with a search engine or on an encyclopedia such as Wikipedia. If your topic is fairly broad but not controversial, you may want to start with books.

Whatever path you choose, as you begin your research process, keep a researcher's journal. (This can be shared with your students and serve as a model for them.) Use this journal to keep track of the information you find, but also be reflective about the process itself. You may want to make it a double-entry journal, recording the information you found in one column and your commentary in the other. Your commentary should include things like:

- How you found the source
- Why you decided the source was credible
- What perspective(s) are represented in the source
- How this information compares to other information you've read on your topic
- What additional questions this information inspires
- What (for complex or technical texts) strategies you used to comprehend the source

Write about the choices you made: When did you switch from getting oriented to really digging for information? How did you decide if something was credible or not? Where were your dead ends or frustration points? What did you do when you couldn't find information? What did you do when information was too technical or above your expertise? Your process will be something to draw upon when you teach this process to your students.

DO YOU NEED A GUIDE?

In addition to getting oriented through reading, expert generalists also turn to guides, people who help them make sense of the territory. Remember that guides can come from lots of different places: libraries, museums, government agencies, nonprofits, local college, or even your colleagues. Think of a guide as someone who knows the terrain, even if they don't know everything about the topic you are pursuing.

Expert generalists don't *always* need guides during their information-seeking project—they use guides when they are looking into very specialized or technical fields (for example, legal cases or cutting-edge science). Sometimes they need a guide to help them get started—to even decide what stories to cover—but other times guides are consulted when expert generalists run into challenges with their reading. One of the biggest lessons we took from these experts is how collaborative research is (or could be)—and how important having face-to-face conversations is to the process.

Finding a Guide

Look at your topic and your general background reading again—do you need a guide to help you make sense of the field and direct you to credible sources or interesting angles on your topic? Brainstorm a list of potential guides, people you know or could connect with personally, and choose one or two that you could contact. Next, consider what you would like your guide to help you with. Do you have a source that is confusing that you need help reading? Do you want to know if your topic seems worth pursuing? Do you want to know if there are any community resources available on your topic in the local community? Do you want to know if your guide could point you to specific journals or connect you with individual experts? Prepare yourself and then reach out to your potential guide with your questions. Keep track of what happens in your researcher's journal.

MOTIVATION AND INTEREST

Finally, getting oriented is also an opportunity to test the waters and see if a broad area is something you're even interested in at all. Some topics sound appealing at first, but once you begin looking at a few resources you may realize that your interest simply isn't there. When your research is high stakes—when you're preparing to vote or investigating something about your health, for example—you will likely persist with your reading and researching even when the information is dry. However, for many classroom investigations, we encourage you to help your students identify a topic or question that is intrinsically motivating. This might mean that students will change topics after some initial reading. That's often perfectly fine. As a teacher, you'll want to keep an eye out for students who use topic changing as a form of procrastination, but in many cases (and within reason) changing topics early on in the process is perfectly acceptable—and may result in higher engagement and deeper learning.

A Flirtation or Something More?

Alexandria was a master's student in Angela's Teaching Nonfiction Writing course who had to engage in her own multiweek information-seeking project. At the beginning of the semester, she completed the brainstorming activity outlined in the Finding a Topic box, page 58. Her questions ranged from those about her new teaching job (Will the administration be supportive? How will I handle the commute?) to questions about her lack of gardening skills (Why haven't my avocado pits started growing? Why do I have a black thumb?).

When asked to choose a topic for her project, Alexandria selected gardening. After all, she was genuinely interested in getting something to grow on her balcony and the project seemed like a good opportunity to figure out how. She got to work, but the project wasn't any fun. Reluctantly, she set out to research plants that might grow in her part of Florida, but her heart wasn't in it.

A few days later, she happened to have a conversation with a waiter at a restaurant where she was dining. He shared that he and a friend had a bee colony. This happenstance conversation reminded her of something she'd heard a while ago and always wanted to learn more about: the declining honeybee population. Knowing that her project had to be narrow and focused, she decided to change her topic from gardening to honeybees in Florida. Suddenly she went from dreading the project to enthusiastically reading everything she could. As she later reflected: "I scratched my work and started from the beginning . . . I followed the [same] planning strategies, but this time, I was fascinated by my research! I wanted to read and read about my topic. I experienced a very important lesson firsthand: interest plays a huge role in motivation."

The takeaway is this: there was nothing intrinsically more valuable in a student learning about honeybees versus learning about gardening. The only one who knows that one topic is "better" than the other is the student herself.

Assessing Your Progress

Now that you've done some orienting and researching, take stock of where you are. Review your notes from your research, and then consider the following questions:

- What is the most interesting thing you've learned so far about your topic?
- Have you answered your initial question? If so, are you satisfied with your answer? Where else could you look to deepen your understanding? If you haven't, where might you turn next?
- What new questions or curiosities has your reading and research inspired? Which, if any, of these might be worth pursuing?
- How might you narrow your thinking so you can research in more detail?

Your goal at this point is to move from a broad question (or series of questions) or a general topic to something smaller and more focused. Ideally, it will be a topic you can share with your students so you can use yourself as a classroom model.

Chapter 6

EVALUATING SOURCES

Orienting yourself to a new topic helps you get the lay of the (informational) land. You learn important background knowledge that may help you move from a very broad topic or question to something more focused. You may even change your topic as you gain orienting information. But at some point, if you are to engage in a focused information-seeking quest, you need to move from gathering general, orienting information to a deep dive search. In this chapter, you'll learn how generalists think about the information they encounter.

> **Staying Organized**
>
> Staying organized when you do research can be a challenge. There are many tools for keeping track of your sources of information, from analog (index cards, journals) to digital (bookmarking tools, Google classroom, etc.). As you continue on your information-seeking journey, experiment with different tools. Remember that your process will be a useful model for your students. Sharing your real challenges—as well as your strategies for persisting—can be wonderful teaching moments.

When we talked with expert generalists, we recognized that one of their most important skills was the ability to identify credible sources and dig for information beyond the superficial. This process involved online resources as well as archival resources and first-person interviews. (See Chapter 7 for information about the types of sources, including interviews.) No matter where they got their information, though, they considered several interlocking factors:

- Is this source *credible*? What does it mean to be credible in this instance? (Some generalists also kept track of less-than-credible sources to describe myths or common misconceptions about a topic.)

- How does the concept of *expertise* relate to this source? Am I directly accessing expert information, or has expert information been consulted to create this source?

- Is this *source* primary, secondary, or tertiary? In other words, how close am I to the information itself? How much does that matter?

- What *perspective* does this source have in relationship to my question? Do I need more than one perspective to answer my question?

- Is this source deliberately *biased* or designed to *manufacture doubt* about this topic?

In this chapter, we'll explore the first two concepts, credibility and expertise. In the next chapter, we'll talk about types of sources and perspectives.

Biases and Hoaxes

- In this text, we use the term *perspective* to refer to the point of view all people and sources bring to a topic. We teach students to consider the perspective or point of view of *all* sources as a regular habit of mind.
- We also recognize that some sources are extremely skewed or are deliberately designed to manufacture doubt about issues where expert consensus actually exists. These we will refer to as "biased"—and we encourage students to learn to avoid them when investigating important or high-stakes topics. They can do so by opening a new tab and searching for more information about the site's sponsor or by checking information provided against known credible sources and/or fact-checking websites (see Mike Caulfield's [2017] helpful blog for more on how to do this).
- Finally, we know that everyone, even expert generalists, may be fooled by a well-designed hoax or deceptive online story. This book isn't about never getting tricked—but it is about thinking carefully about the information you encounter.

CREDIBILITY AND EXPERTISE

A key generalist skill is the ability to ask good questions of appropriate sources. In other words, generalists know who (or what) to consult and what to ask. This skill is connected directly to an understanding of credibility and expertise, two concepts that need untangling.

In this context, the word *credible* means reasonable to trust or believe. Notice that *credible* isn't synonymous with *true*. A credible source may later turn out to be wrong. This doesn't mean that the source wasn't credible, but new information may turn out to be better or different than what was initially thought/predicted/written.

If a credible source is one that you can *reasonably believe*, what makes it *reasonable* to believe a source?

One of the first criteria you might use to evaluate a source is related to the concept of *expertise*. In the information age, people must rely on the thinking and understanding of experts all the time. Eva Thomm and Rainer Bromme (2012) describe this as a "division of cognitive labor"—no one can become an expert in every area necessary to navigate the modern world. In our work with teachers, we like to refer to this as a need to off-load credibility judgments to someone or something else. There are better and worse ways to do this, of course. You could off-load decisions about diet to product advertisements or to your doctor. When a decision is important, you will want to get expert perspectives—perspectives that come from people with training and/or experience (often both) related to the topic at hand.

Sometimes you might access experts directly. You could conduct interviews or send emails. You might visit the doctor, go to the auto mechanic, have a plumber look at the stopped drain. In these cases, you are getting their expertise unfiltered—you are interacting with a primary source.

Some sources are absolutely, positively *not* credible, and, once you learn to recognize them, you don't turn to them when you need information. Some sources are out to spread misinformation to get you to buy things you don't need or do things against your own self-interest. Remember that *credibility* is not synonymous with *true*—even sources that are not credible might be correct every once in a while. But you can probably think of instances when you've encountered an obviously bad source—a quack doctor, an aggressive salesperson, an incompetent plumber—and, subsequently, have decided to avoid using their services or accessing their "expertise." Recent world events have shed light on just how many bad sources of information are online—and how difficult these can be to spot. It is easier to learn to recognize (and turn to) credible sources than it is to ferret out all the bad sources of information, which is the approach we take in our own lives and in our teaching.

Learning to rely on credible sources doesn't mean memorizing a set of decontextualized rules—rules like "Trust all websites that end in .edu" or "Use the CRAP (currency/relevance/accuracy/perspective) test to evaluate websites." These rules don't treat credibility as nuanced (and, quite frankly, some of the checklists take forever to go through). In practice, when you are actually looking for information, most sources aren't simply credible or not credible—instead, credibility is a function of the question at hand. The auto mechanic you used to rely on doesn't work on hybrids so you need to look for a new auto shop now that you bought a Prius. The first mechanic is still a credible source of information for all kinds of car issues, just not this one.

So, step one in accessing a credible primary source of information (we'll get into secondary sources—online and in journalism—a bit later) is to determine whether or not the source is an expert on the issue/question/problem that you're interested in.

This may be the only step you take. One really expert source of information may turn out to be plenty for the question you have. However, often we need *multiple* credible sources of information to address our needs. Why?

As we touched on in Chapter 4, there are different reasons to access more than one source of information. Some of these reasons are unrelated to the seriousness of the question or topic (you might simply like to read about your favorite sports team from different angles, even enjoying really biased sources that make you feel good about being a fan). Other times, though, your information needs mean that you absolutely *must* access multiple, credible sources of information to answer your questions well. Helping students understand when (and why) more than one source is needed is a key part of supporting generalist literacy.

We argue that multiple expert/credible sources of information are *mandatory* in the following instances:

- When the stakes are high or the information need is serious *and*
- When the issue is uncertain and/or unsettled, even among experts

Of course, you may choose to access multiple sources of information for all kinds of information-seeking needs beyond these. Teaching students to become expert generalists will give them the skills to access multiple credible sources any time they wish—but if both of the preceding statements are true, you simply must look at multiple good sources if you wish to be well informed and/or make good choices.

You may be in a situation where you need to access more than one source of information to meet a variety of different information needs. More than one source of information can provide you with:

- Corroboration or verification of facts (necessary if you can't get to the original source of information and/or the facts are disputed)
- Context (somewhat like orienting info—backing away from the issue at hand to see it from a larger angle)
- Consensus
- Different perspectives, including:
    - Insider expert (such as the scientists who did the experiment, employees of the company, or members of a particular organization or group affected by the issue)
    - Outsider expert (specialists in the same field who did not do the experiment, employees of a competitor, members of a related organization)
    - Stakeholders (people who have the condition that the new scientific breakthrough would treat, consumers, members of the general public)
- Answers to different kinds of questions

Scenarios as a Teaching Tool

Scenarios are a great tool to explore issues with students. Begin by familiarizing students with the format of a scenario: here's the problem, what could it mean? What possible actions does each result suggest? Generalist thinking is often about risk assessment and gathering the information you need to make a decision.

Try this scenario yourself and then consider how you might modify it for use with your students.

Imagine this: You don't feel very good. You've been feeling pretty bad for a while now—going on a week—and you're starting to wonder what's wrong. You've accessed some nonexperts for their advice (your mom, your significant other, neither of whom work in the medical field), and they've given you some nonexpert advice (get rest, drink more fluids, take an ibuprofen), but their advice doesn't help—you still feel rotten. You finally decide to make an appointment with your doctor.

You've reached step one: you're accessing a credible source of information. You consider your primary care doctor a credible source because their expertise (medical degree, years of experience in primary care) lines up with the problem and questions you perceive yourself to have.

At this point, let's consider three possible outcomes to this doctor's visit and how you might move forward from each.

Possible Outcome 1: *You have a cold.* It turns out that your mom and your significant other were right—you just need some more rest and more fluids. As a matter of fact, by the time you got to the appointment, you were already feeling a little better and you suspected the problem was on its way to resolving itself.

When the doctor diagnoses a cold and sympathetically tells you there's a particularly bad one going around, do you accept this diagnosis? Are you content accessing only one source of information?

(continues)

(continued)

If you're like us, yes. But why? We're guessing here, but you probably accept this diagnosis for a combination of the following reasons:

1. Your doctor has training and experience in this area.
2. You may have had previous experiences with this doctor, and they have been correct before.
3. You may have a relationship with your doctor that adds an emotional dimension—you want to trust this person.
4. The answer aligns with your expectations and hopes.
5. The solution is simple.
6. The stakes do not feel very high.

To start with, you probably accept the diagnosis because the doctor is a credible source of information. Your significant other kept telling you it was just a cold, but you weren't satisfied with the same answer from a nonexpert. Good for you. You wanted a credible opinion.

But, in accepting your doctor's diagnosis, you likely used more than just logical thinking. Emotionally, you like your doctor. You also don't really want to have a serious health problem so you're happy to have a simple diagnosis. Because you've started to feel better, the stakes also seem pretty low. Even if it isn't a cold, what difference does it really make? You're almost better anyway.

Possible Outcome 2: *You have a chronic condition and need medication.* But what if your doctor does not say "cold"? Let's make the situation just a little more complicated and think about what happens next.

This time, the doctor looks at your stuffy nose and watery eyes and hears you describe your symptoms and concludes that you have seasonal allergies, made worse because you just moved to a place where allergies can be very, very bad (and where the pollen season goes on forever!). After discussing your health history around this issue, the doctor wants you to try a daily pill to control your symptoms.

This diagnosis isn't life shattering, but it's a little more complicated than the first possible outcome. It may not be what you were hoping to hear. The stakes may feel a little higher, especially if the allergy pill being prescribed isn't covered by your insurance or comes with unwanted side effects.

Do you seek multiple sources of information for this issue, or is a single source enough?

Most of us might not go to a second doctor at this point—we might not seek out multiple sources on the initial question (What's wrong with me?). The doctor you're talking with still seems like a credible source based on training, experience, and your own previous encounters with the doctor. But you may want more than one source to understand this particular problem and potential solution.

After asking your doctor a few questions about the prescription and what you might expect, you head home. When you get there, you realize you still have more questions. These new questions were inspired by the answer to the first question (What's wrong with me? Allergies.) and might call for different kinds of expertise. You might ask your friend who you know has allergies whether they take a prescription and, if so, how it makes them feel. You might do a little investigating online, reading about side effects or alternative medicine. You might call someone (your insurance company, your significant other) about the cost of the medicine.

In the end, you'll have to take some action. Take the prescription, live with the allergies, or try an alternate treatment. Pay out of pocket or make repeated phone calls to the insurance company.

The stakes still aren't terribly high, and how much information you seek out will probably depend on how much time and/or money you have, how badly you feel, and how concerned you are about the long-term consequences of daily medication versus the long-term consequences of feeling rotten (a version of the cost–benefit analysis that guides many of our life decisions).

(continues)

(continued)

The lesson from this scenario is that multiple sources are sometimes necessary to answer different kinds of questions. Your original question was answered by the first credible source—the doctor—and you're not all that worried about *corroborating* the diagnosis. Your question about how the medication feels may be answered by someone who takes it (an expert by virtue of experiences); your question about long-term consequences may require you to read some health websites (all secondary sources—see Chapter 7 for more about the types of sources); your question about generic equivalents and what your insurance covers will need to be answered by the insurance company or its website. Each source you consult must be evaluated for credibility and expertise related to the particular question you have (the drug manufacturer is required to list the side effects, for example, but also may minimize them—both figuratively and literally, through small font or placement on a website—because of a desire to sell the medicine).

Possible Outcome 3: *That cough? Maybe something serious.* Now, though, consider the worst possible outcome, one that might come after the initial visit and diagnosis doesn't seem quite right. You're still not feeling well weeks, even months later. You go back a second time and get some tests. Maybe you go back a third time, and your primary care doctor decides that you need to be referred to a specialist. At this point in time, your doctor no longer has the expertise necessary to treat your condition. Your question—What's wrong with me?—is now outside their training and experience.

You get an appointment with the specialist and eventually you get some complicated and unwelcome news. Let's be clear—the specialist is a credible source of information. The specialist has the appropriate expertise to diagnose your condition. But do you accept this single source of information, or do you look for multiple sources? If you seek out multiple sources, why do you do so?

Emotions play a big role in medical diagnoses of this nature, of course. If the stakes are very high—if this is life and death—you really want the best information you can find. As you confront this situation—or other life-changing situations that are less drastic (How does a balloon mortgage work? Should I sign up for the pension or the 403(b) retirement plan?)—you have all kinds of questions that call for all kinds of different expertise.

Before you get any further, you may want to *corroborate/verify* the specialist's diagnosis by getting a second opinion. *Corroboration* is the most basic reason we may access multiple sources. You might decide to consult a second source to verify/corroborate the specialist's diagnosis when some of the following conditions are present:

1. You doubt the doctor's expertise or training in the area.
2. You don't trust the doctor because of a lack of an emotional connection/relationship.
3. The diagnosis does not align with your expectations or hopes.
4. The condition is hard to diagnose and/or diagnosis criteria are controversial or uncertain.
5. The solution to the diagnosis is very complicated and unwanted.
6. The stakes are high.

You go to another doctor to get a second opinion to see if the second doctor agrees or disagrees with the first.

If, though, the diagnostic criteria are straightforward or you have confidence in the initial diagnosis, you still may seek a second opinion (a second source) to figure out your treatment options. You may want to *corroborate* the treatment plan you've been given by your doctor by asking a second doctor or by doing further research (going online to medical websites and patient blogs, talking to people you know who have this condition or who are in the medical field, etc.). You may also be looking for an *alternate* treatment plan, especially if you really, really don't like the plan that's been prescribed, if the stakes seem very high, or if the disease is quite rare or complicated. You may want multiple sources to confirm/corroborate or disagree with the treatment plan if it entails something life-threatening or changing before you move forward.

(continues)

(continued)

Let's stop and take note of those two reasons for seeking multiple sources of information:

- To corroborate/verify information
- To explore multiple/alternate perspectives on an issue

As in the allergies scenario, you may also seek multiple sources of information because of *new questions* inspired by the answer to the first question (What's wrong with me?). Each of these new questions may require different kinds of expertise to answer them. You'll need to access new sources—and to think about their credibility—as new questions appear. Here are just a few questions I might have if I received a difficult medical diagnosis:

- What is this disease exactly? How does it work? What's happening to me?
- What exactly will treatment entail?
- What does treatment *feel* like?
- Does insurance cover treatment?
- What lifestyle changes will (or should) happen in conjunction with treatment?
- Is anyone available for emotional support?

Your specialist may or may not be a credible source of information to answer these questions. She was a very good source for diagnosis and, perhaps, treatment, but some of the questions above call for different kinds of expertise (expertise rooted in experiences and/or training, sometimes both). Each question may require you to seek out a new source of information, a source that may or may not need to be corroborated with additional sources.

For some of these questions, you might be able to find first-person, primary sources to talk with. You might call the insurance company, ask for a longer appointment with the doctor, seek out support groups at the hospital. However, you will probably also head online to find primary and secondary sources there, too. Many complex information needs are answered though both *in-person sources* and *online sources.*

Matching Questions and Sources

As you continue investigating your topic in more detail, brainstorm *the kinds of experts* you have accessed (or hope to access) and the kinds of questions each is equipped to answer. You may wish to create a chart, like the one below based on Gamal's research into type 2 diabetes. (See Chapter 3 for more on Gamal's research project.)

Gamal's Source Chart		
Type of Expertise	**Potential Source**	**Possible Questions the Source Could Answer**
First person/ stakeholder	People with type 2 diabetes (ideally more than one)	• When were you diagnosed? What does diabetes feel like? How has it changed your life? What would you tell someone else who just got diagnosed?
Expert: Medical doctor: general practitioner	Grandmother's doctor, website reviewed by medical professionals (check more than one)	• How is the disease diagnosed? What is diabetes exactly? • What parts of the body does it affect? • How do different medicines work? • What lifestyle changes should someone with diabetes make?
Expert: Medical doctor: specialist (endocrinologist)	Medical website reviewed by endocrinologist or specialist someone in the class knows	• Are there any other diseases that people with type 2 diabetes are at greater risk for? Where can I find answers to more detailed questions about the biology of the disease?
Expert: Pharmacologist	Medical website; local pharmacist	• How do diabetes medications work? • What are the potential side effects?
Expert: Nutritionist	Medical website; local nutritionists	• What kind of diets are best for people with diabetes? • How does diet help people with diabetes? • Are there any controversies around diets for people with diabetes?
Expert/stakeholders: Advocacy group	American Diabetes Association	• What research is being done on diabetes treatments or cures? How is research funded? • Can I use this website to double-check information found through other sources?

As you continue with your project, be sure to note when your sources disagree with one another—and think about how you decide what information is best when your sources are contradictory.

Remember that assessing credibility is a tricky skill to master. Unless students are taught to think carefully about how they decide what to believe, many people fall back on unreliable cues (such as position on a search results page, number of likes or comments, etc.). Generalists slow down and systematically think about the credibility of the information they consume.

Author, Message, and Source Credibility

In the field of communications, scholars have identified three different levels of credibility that people talk about when they describe why they chose to trust information: author credibility, message/content credibility, and source credibility. What does that mean?

Imagine these student-friendly scenarios:

- A stranger tells you that there is no school tomorrow. Do you believe them? Most kids would say no—the stranger has no *author credibility* on this issue. How would they know? On the other hand, if the principal said there was no school tomorrow, would you believe them? Most kids would say yes. The principal has *high author credibility.*
- On the other hand, the same stranger comes into the classroom and announces there is no school tomorrow on a day when you know there's a blizzard moving in overnight. Do you believe them now? Even though the stranger still has low author credibility, the *message/content* credibility make it more likely that kids will say yes, the stranger is believable.
- Finally, the school website displays a message that says "School is canceled for [tomorrow's date]." Do you believe the message? Most kids would say yes—the *source credibility* is so high that you would be unlikely to wonder who wrote the message or if it's a prank.

These categories are descriptive, not prescriptive—scholars have *not* identified what people *should do* but rather what they *actually do.* The categories can provide you and your students language for talking about credibility in a nuanced way. When students say they believe a source is credible, ask why. Is it (1) because of the person providing the information, (2) because the content makes sense in terms of the context, or (3) or because of where the information came from?

If students point to the *author,* see if you can get them to talk about whether the author is an expert and/or the primary source of the information needed (e.g., the principal is absolutely credible on school closings when the principal is the person in charge of making that determination).

If they suggest the information "sounds right" (i.e., content/message credibility), help them think about what makes the information feel accurate and how they could follow up to be more certain. Message credibility may be the easiest to exploit since it often involves our existing biases and emotions (e.g., if we want to believe there won't be school tomorrow, it may be easier to convince us).

If students say a source is credible because of the website itself (i.e., source credibility), ask them to point to the specific qualities of the source that make them say so—is it peer-reviewed? The original source of the information (e.g., the school website declaring school is closed)? Or are they relying on the domain name (e.g., .edu) without thinking about why that source would be credible for their particular information need?

Chapter 7

NAVIGATING THE LANDSCAPE

As you continue your search for information, you'll likely come across a range of sources, both online and (we hope!) in the real world. In this chapter, we'll discuss how generalists think about these sources as positioned within complex information landscape. You'll also get tips for conducting original interviews, one of the most exciting ways we've found to engage students with real-world experts.

KINDS OF SOURCES: PRIMARY, SECONDARY, TERTIARY

Though you can categorize sources in many different ways (by genre, date of publication, publication medium, etc.), we've chosen to use the designations of *primary*, *secondary*, and *tertiary*, categories that attempt to locate a source in terms of its relationship to the original research, information, or event.

If you think those definitions sound confusing or inexact, we agree. Determining if a source is primary, secondary, or tertiary is not straightforward, and different disciplines categorize sources differently. For example, a presidential tweet about a new piece of economic data could be considered a *primary source* about the president's opinion, while still being a *secondary source* about the economic data itself. A historian might consider newspapers written at the time of the U.S. Civil War primary sources, even though contemporary newspapers are considered secondary sources.

And yet despite the inexact science of categorizing sources, helping students understand the relationship between the *source of information* and the *information itself and its use* is an important task. Teachers and librarians we know find the "information cycle" (see Illinois Library n.d. for an example) a helpful way to help students visualize how information moves into the world. We also use these (admittedly loose) definitions:

> **Primary Sources.** Primary sources are the *original*, the kind of source upon which other writing might be based. In history, a primary source might be an original document (the Bill of Rights, for example, or a diary or a speech). In literature, the primary source is the novel you're studying. Interviews, surveys, or other kinds of original data are considered primary sources. In the sciences, a primary source is the original research article that describes the research for the first time (this research is based on data, of course, and the data have been interpreted by the researcher, which is why these distinctions aren't quite a clean as they might seem at first).
>
> **Secondary Sources.** Secondary sources are interpretations of primary sources. A newspaper article that's based on interviews and other reporting is a secondary source. A literary criticism about a work of literature is a secondary source. Students may access secondary sources when the primary source is too difficult (for example, reading a newspaper account about a new scientific discovery is much easier than reading the original research article).

> **Tertiary Sources.** Tertiary sources usually bring together information from primary and secondary sources and synthesize it all in a way that's easy to understand, such as textbooks and encyclopedias. Tertiary sources as especially valuable for *getting oriented.*

What difference does any of this make? We encourage you to think about whether a source you're reading (or viewing) is primary, secondary, or tertiary because it requires you to consider where that source stands in relationship to the information you are exploring. This kind of knowledge—knowledge about the landscape of information—is a key part of being a generalist. If you are reading a tweet that claims your favorite celebrity was just arrested, you may wonder if it's true or not. You may check to see who tweeted the information, if the information includes a link to a source, and if the linked source is based on original reporting or hearsay. If you're a really big fan, you may even follow the trail longer, to try to see an actual mug shot or the arrest paperwork. You may not realize it, but you're probably internally asking yourself "Who says?" about the information, a question we've had success teaching students to ask as a regular habit. When the answer is a gossip column, you probably react differently than if the answer is a court record.

When the question is somewhat low stakes or trivial, you may not spend a lot of time digging—and you may not worry so much about the results. Yet many times when you have a more important question, you run into a paradox: it is important that you get credible information, but you may not have the background or education to read the primary sources yourself.

For example, if you are about to make a major purchase (say, of a new home), you probably want to get the best information you can before you close the deal. However, understanding such things as the types of mortgages available or the various details of a home inspection report may be quite difficult. Similarly, you may be very invested in environmental policy yet not be able to understand the original water quality studies that various organizations have produced in support of (or opposing) a local ballot initiative. In these cases, you may need to access secondary sources—an online explanation of different kinds of mortgages or a newspaper article explaining the water studies—or even tertiary sources to get oriented. You may also turn to *guides*, or real people you know and trust who have expertise in the general area.

The kinds of issues that interest us the most are these: the instances in which you need facts *and* unbiased expert opinions about those facts. High-quality secondary sources (those that gather multiple perspectives, put information into context, leave trails back to *their* sources, and publish corrections when necessary) are often the best sources for these kinds of issues.

Geography Matter

Just because a secondary source is high quality doesn't mean it won't have an editorial point of view or a perspective. For many newspaper stories, one of the most important questions journalists help answer for their readers is, How big of a deal is this? When the news story is about a political topic or a current event, the answer will often depend upon geography. Geography also matters to many science stories (sea level rise is a much bigger deal to residents of Miami, for example, than it is to those living in Boise). If you are investigating a current event or scientific issue, consider accessing secondary sources from different parts of the country or even the world. How does the source's location change the coverage? (See Appendix E for possible sources of information and lesson ideas to try with students.)

PERSPECTIVE

Determining if a source is primary, secondary, or tertiary helps you locate the source of information in relationship to the research, event, or information. But all sources, even primary sources, are created from a particular perspective. This is why generalists are skeptical, why they dig for information, why they consult multiple sources, and why they constantly monitor their progress.

Perspective is distinct from credibility. To think about how, let's consider a few different examples.

First, you are on the National Archives website researching the Civil War and begin to look at photographs taken by Matthew Brady. The National Archives is an extremely credible source of information, and you are very confident that the photographs you are viewing are *actually* photographs taken by Matthew Brady during the Civil War. (They have not been manipulated via any photo-editing software; they are not from some other war; they are not computer-generated images.) The photographs can be *believed* as photographs of the Civil War, but they still must be viewed critically. You will still think carefully about Brady's perspective on his subjects (what he chose to highlight and to minimize, what was just outside the frame, who was in the picture and who wasn't) and the purpose of the photographs in general (Why were they commissioned? Who published them and for what reason? What role did they play at the time?).

In another instance, you might be looking at an original scientific research study. It was published in a peer-reviewed article and, thus, is considered a primary source. There is not much dispute that *at the time of the publication* this research was considered credible. (Note that it may have been refuted or retracted after publication, something you'll only know with more digging.) However, despite its scholarly writing style, the article still reflects the perspective of the authors. You can probably assume that the authors want the information to be construed as important. Good scholars will not overstate their claims—they rarely will use words like *prove* since new information may well change an interpretation. Meanwhile, they will draw conclusions, based on their (credible) perspectives. If it's very important to you to know whether or not their conclusions represent a consensus among scientists or are outside the mainstream (and, perhaps, even refuted by later work), you'll want to seek out other perspectives on the research, by looking for journalistic articles or reviews reporting on the study. (Typically journalists interview other experts who were not involved in the work to offer additional perspectives.) You may also wish to find subsequent articles that cited this article to see if it was accepted or refuted by later work. Always look at publication dates.

Finally, say you are considering purchasing a laptop and are doing a little research on which one to buy. A manufacturer's website is the primary source of information for questions about data storage, compatibility, and so on—and, thus, would be considered credible. Yet the manufacturer definitely has a perspective on the product. If all you want are technical details, reading the manufacturer's site may be enough; however, you may also want to access unbiased product reviews on other websites before you make a purchase.

Your Information Map

As you continue collecting information about your topic, plot your sources of information on the information landscape and consider the perspectives you have represented (see the example below, using Gamal's research). As we noted previously, this is tricky! Just because a source is primary doesn't mean it represents an expert perspective. Just because a source represents an expert point of view doesn't mean it's still considered credible. Although this may make your head spin at first, remember that generalists are persistent and committed to accuracy and that this process becomes more familiar with practice. Generalists also know when to stop—when they've gotten the most complete look at an issue that they need (or have time to pursue).

Topic: The Impact of Diabetes on Everyday Life			
Type of Expertise	**Primary Sources**	**Secondary Sources**	**Tertiary Sources**
How Can This Expertise Be Accessed?	• Interviews with people with diabetes (first-person perspective) • Interview with grandmother's general practitioner (medical expert, general) • Interview with pharmacist (medication expert) • Interview with classmate's mother, a nutritionist (dietary expert)	• Newspaper article about diabetes and exercise (includes quotes from medical doctors, people with diabetes, and exercise physiologists, along with background information) • Magazine interview with a nutritionist about dietary concerns for diabetics • Newspaper article about a new drug for diabetes patients (includes interviews with an endocrinologist and a pharmacologist)	• WebMD.com, kidshealth.org, and MayoClinic.org (all are reviewed by medical doctors) • American Diabetes Association website (https://www.diabetes.org/) for general background information and to double-check facts on other sites

THE POWER OF THE INTERVIEW

If you look at Gamal's chart in the "Considering the Information Landscape" box, you probably notice something about the primary sources he is planning to use: they are all interviews. An interview is one of the best ways for students to gather primary research on topics they find fascinating (surveys, created and distributed with online tools, are another exciting possibility and have the benefit of sharpening math skills). Other types of primary sources may be difficult to access (or, once accessed, difficult to read)—but most students can successfully interview an expert or stakeholder. Interviews also have the important benefit of preparing students to talk with adults (or, in the case of emailed interviews, to write to adults).

Although connecting with experts has never been easier, students (and adults) need some help to do a good job. Don't just tell your students (no matter how old they are!) that they need to do an interview and assume that they'll figure it out. Inundating experts with emailed questions that show little evidence of preparation can even create ill will—many experts are really busy people! At best, your students may get a form letter (often the case with public figures such as a senator) or no response at all.

Although there's no surefire way to get an expert to respond to an interview request, there are ways to improve your chances, while also teaching students valuable skills.

An Expert Writes Back

A student in Dr. Buerger's class emailed a highly regarded researcher with questions about the skin condition eczema. Not only did the researcher reply (with detailed answers to her questions), he encouraged her to pursue a career in medicine herself one day. At the end of his note, he added the following:

> PS My daughter will enter middle school next year. I hope she will be as curious and industrious as you appear to be when the time comes.

You will find some of Dr. Buerger's tips for getting experts to respond to student writers in Appendix I.

The Importance of Stuff

As part of a journalist-in-training project, we distributed press passes for students to wear when they were conducting interviews. These press passes were pretty simple: a plastic card with our project's logo, worn on a lanyard. Yet the students and their teachers loved them! Every student who had an article published in the paper was given a press pass to keep—and these passes became badges of honor in many classrooms.

Enclothed Cognition

This press pass experience reminds us of the work of Hajo Adam and Adam D. Galinsky (2012), two psychologists who developed a theory of "enclothed cognition." Their studies were designed to test the hypothesis that wearing a lab coat described as a "doctor's coat" would increase the wearer's careful and sustained attention—and it did! Study participants who wore the coat performed better on tasks requiring attention and memory than those who did not. Even more fascinating, participants who wore the coat performed better than those who (1) saw the coat in a picture but didn't wear it or (2) wore the same coat but were told it was a "painter's coat." Their resulting theory stated that clothes will have an impact on a wearer if the clothes:

- Have symbolic meaning to the wearer
- Are physically worn

Classroom Connections

What does this enclothed cognition theory mean for teachers, especially those working toward generalist literacy? Let's start with the first principle: if the clothing or object has *symbolic meaning to the wearer, it can affect student identity and action.*

Many teachers intuitively know this. Some ask students to dress up on days they give a presentation or have an important test, hoping that professional dress will lead to professionalism in other ways (cognitively and behaviorally). Yet professional dress doesn't always make much difference in students' performance, perhaps because the definition of *dressing up* and the symbolic meaning of the clothing students choose to wear may not be the same for students as what the teacher had in mind.

The second principle is also important: the object or clothes need to *physically* be part of the student's repertoire. Showing students the press pass (or even the physical magazine) didn't change the way they thought or behaved, but students who *wore* the passes acted like real reporters.

As you work to create a generalist literacy identity within students, we encourage you to remember these principles and experiment with clothing (we suspect it may also work with objects, tools, even physical arrangement of space). Work together as a class to endow the clothing and other objects with symbolic meaning. If you choose to produce a project as part of your generalist literacy instruction—a class newsmagazine, a series of children's books, or a set of library displays—consider how you might add symbolic value to the realia (in the form of clothes, objects, tools, signage, or alterations to the physical space) in your environment.

WHO SHOULD YOU INTERVIEW?

The first step is to locate someone to interview. It is often more fruitful to contact someone local than to reach out to an international or national figure that you've come across in a newspaper article (although this isn't always true—as in the vignette in the "Classroom Vignette" box). Who you should interview also depends on your topic. If you are researching something unusual, the world's foremost expert may be eager to learn their research has a following. But if you're interested in how the iPhone works, contacting the CEO of Apple is unlikely to get a response.

Consider the following possibilities when looking for experts to interview:

- The class (We encourage students to share their research process regularly with one another so that everyone can draw on the community's contacts and connections.)
- Your sphere of friends and family, including colleagues at the school
- Local businesses or service providers (Your personal pharmacists, physical therapist, dentist, car mechanic, etc. may be willing to talk about their areas of expertise with your students—or they may know someone else who can.)

- Your local university or community college (Many universities have a public relations department that can assist with identifying experts who are willing to be interviewed.)

- Local nonprofits and government organizations (Museums, librarians, public offices, and advocacy groups often have public outreach services.)

Be creative as you consider the perspectives that will add value to an information-seeking quest. Students often forget the expertise that's all around them—a parent who has worked in landscaping for years may be a great source for information about starting a school garden, even if they don't have an advanced degree (and is probably a much *better* source that a university professor who lives a thousand miles away).

WHAT QUESTIONS SHOULD YOU ASK?

Never conduct an interview—even over email—without preparing for it first. Background reading is essential. Read as much as you can about the topic you're researching before you interview, and, if possible, also learn what you can about the person herself. You don't want to ask questions that you could have easily found by doing a simple Google search—and your questions need to be things that the person is suited to answer (not things outside his or her expertise). If you get confused while doing your background reading, you may be able to ask your interviewee to clarify. Experts are always impressed with well-thought-out questions!

HOW SHOULD QUESTIONS BE WORDED AND ORDERED?

After you've done your background reading, it's time to write your questions. Avoid yes-or-no questions and multipart questions. Don't write too many questions, especially if you are going to send them over email (three is probably enough). If the interview will be in person or over the phone, rank your questions by importance in case you run out of time.

Alan Newman, one of our favorite science journalists, recommends ending every interview with the question, "Is there anything else you think I should know?" (Saul et al. 2012, 112) or some version of this. This question allows the interviewee to add additional details that the interviewer may not have even known to ask. It can even open up a whole new conversation!

WHAT SHOULD YOU DO DURING THE INTERVIEW?

The most important thing to do during an interview is *listen*. Careful listening allows you to ask additional questions based on what the person is telling you. Don't be afraid to deviate from your question list! This is the advantage of talking with someone directly, as opposed to getting information from the Internet or a book. Also, don't be intimidated by big words or technical jargon—ask your interviewee to explain what these words mean.

In addition to careful listening, we also advise students to take good notes during an interview. These can be messy, incomplete sentences that will later be typed up (ideally, right after the interview, before memory fades). If possible, the interview can also be recorded, as long as the interviewee gives permission. If you eventually want to write about your investigation, you should quote the person directly only if you've written down or recorded their exact words.

Finally, if you plan to use your interview in any kind of writing or presentation, be sure be sure to confirm the spelling of the person's name and degree (if applicable), along with pertinent background information (for example, you may want to know or confirm the specific name of his job title, along with number of years in the field).

Conduct an Interview

After reading the previous tips, select someone to interview for your project. Follow this process:

- Brainstorm a list of potential people to interview and select one.
- Review your research and conduct additional background reading to prepare.
- Write a list of questions and rank your questions in order of importance.
- Contact the expert and ask if he or she would be willing to talk with you. Arrange a time to talk on the phone or in person. If necessary, send a list of questions via email.
- If you receive no response, try another person on your list. Be persistent! Consider tapping into your personal and professional networks to find someone who is willing.
- Conduct the interview and take notes. Type your notes when you're finished. If you recorded the interview, listen to the recording and add to your notes.

When you are finished, reflect on the process. What went well? What were your challenges? How did you overcome the challenges? What would you do differently next time? How will you use your own interview process in your classroom?

The Whole-Class Interview

The first time you assign an interview to your students, you may want to do the interview as a whole class. These interviews can be about a particular curricular topic that you are already studying or they can arise from a whole-class investigation (remember, generalist literacy skills can be fostered through whole-class, small-group, and individual investigations). You may also find a way to connect whole-class interviews to school or grade-level guest speakers who are already scheduled. Ask your principal or grade-level leader if the speaker can leave time at the end of her presentation to answer student questions. Finally, field trips may offer yet another opportunity to conduct a whole-class interview. Once again, arrange for time for student questions as part of the field trip agenda.

In the case of whole-class interviews, follow the same procedures outlined in the "Conduct an Interview" box, with a few variations. Together with your students, brainstorm specific people and/or perspectives you'd like to access. Once you have a list, talk together about how you might contact such experts. This may be an opportunity to introduce students to local organizations and institutions that they may not otherwise encounter; it also may be a chance for students in the class to share connections they have. (If a guest speaker or field trip has already been scheduled, help students think about why the speaker has been invited and what perspectives they may bring.)

Once you've chosen an expert to interview, invite them to the class, either in person or via videoconference. Help students do background reading to prepare for the interview; in small groups, ask them to brainstorm a list of potential questions. Compile all the group's questions into a class-wide list (you may wish to put all the questions together into a single list yourself so you can easily eliminate duplicates) and, with the class, rank the questions in order from most important to least.

On the day of the interview, you can act as the moderator, asking the class's questions yourself. (Many actual organizations conduct press conferences this way, with all questions funneled through a single moderator. Some political debates also use this format.) Be sure students are taking notes during the process. The next day, discuss what you learned, what (if any) follow-up questions you have, and what you want to know next. Also give students an opportunity to think about the choices you made as a moderator: Did you ask a follow-up question not on the list? Why? Did you reorder the questions during the interview? How did you know when to ask the next question and when to let the guest keep talking? (See Appendix F for a classroom example.)

Books in the Internet Age

If you want to know answers to straightforward factual questions, the best place to go is the Internet. It's efficient and the information on, for example, whether *all* spiders have eight legs, what spiders eat, or how they function as both predators and prey is almost surely reliable and easily available. But sometimes you don't want to know simple factual information—sometimes you want *more.* This is where books come in. Books today have a different function than even a few years ago. In fact, that function may be even more important today. But we need to make that function explicit to young people (and to parents who may wonder whether purchasing a computer or software is a smarter budget decision than buying books) by offering them examples that prove this point.

Books—engaging, thought-provoking, well-designed books—do more than provide information. Here we are *not* talking about the workmanlike "readers" that have been produced to help students practice reading skills and learn some facts. No, a good book does more. It might give shape to a topic by helping readers to understand the issues that an expert on the subject sees as pertinent. It may provoke the readers' curiosity. It might model creative and critical thinking. It might discuss how a question changes over time and how research has changed what we now know. It might be clever and even offer a humorous take on the subject. A quick Internet search isn't going to do any of this. The best books will always do more than simply provide information, and our students deserve opportunities to delight in such books.

Then there are questions about the designation "nonfiction" itself. What, for instance, might young readers learn about survival skills by reading a Gary Paulson or Jean Craighead George novel? Such novels not only provide information but also offer students a memorable story, a narrative that may well change the way they look at "facts." Does a book like *Balloons over Broadway,* which offers a true story but employs a structure and voice noticeably different than an easily classified nonfiction book that helps young readers identify rocks and minerals, count as informational text? Are books illustrated with photographs more realistic than interpretive illustrations? (A scientific illustrator would surely disagree if you said yes to that question!)

The bottom line here: books are definitely important, but it is important to think about the special opportunities they invite and what they don't do particularly well. Requiring student researchers to find "one book and three websites" masks the important differences between books and the Internet (while also treating all information on the Internet as equal).

Chapter 8

POWERING THROUGH TO THE END

Let's review what you've done so far in this self-guided course. If you've come this far, you've:

- Identified a general topic that's interesting to you
- Gotten oriented to your topic by doing background reading
- Narrowed your focus to a specific question or series of questions
- Deeply pursued those questions by reading credible sources from a variety of perspectives
- Evaluated all sources, knowing that both accuracy and credibility are contextual
- Identified an expert to interview; prepared for and conducted an interview
- Kept careful notes of what you're learning

Along the way, you may have run into trouble: sources that you had trouble evaluating, questions that were difficult to answer, contradictory information, potential experts who wouldn't return emails or phone calls. Developing persistence in the face of these challenges is a key generalist literacy goal.

Reflective Journal

Reflect on the challenges from your information-seeking process and the strategies you used when you faced a challenge (even if the strategies were not successful). What did you learn about developing persistence from your experience? Spend some time freewriting on persistence in information seeking.

When you are finished freewriting, review what you wrote. We think of a generalist identity as comprising ways *doing, knowing, and being.* Based on your experiences, what did you learn about:

- The generalist's ways of doing:
  - How to use specific search strategies or websites
  - Internet shortcuts or techniques (i.e., copying and pasting a Web URL into a new search bar; opening a new tab)
  - Interview techniques
- The generalist's ways of knowing:
  - Knowledge of reliable sources for particular subjects
  - Knowledge of local organizations or institutions where experts can be accessed
  - Knowledge of the landscape of information as related to your topic
- The generalist's ways of being:
  - Curious
  - Skeptical
  - Persistent

WHAT NEXT? SHARING WHAT WE'VE LEARNED

If you've been truly interested in your search topic, chances are you've also been sharing what you're learning as you go. You may have mentioned your project to a friend or coworker. You may have even shared links on social media or via email. Students will do the same thing. As long as they are invested in their searches, they'll usually be eager to share what they've learned. The trick, as a teacher, is to determine what kind of sharing makes the most sense.

First, think broadly. Sharing does not need to be a written product or formal presentation. If you teach generalist literacy skills only in the context of formal projects, students will never acquire generalist literacy. They just won't have enough opportunities to practice.

For smaller questions and investigations, students might orally share their learning, either as part of a regular sharing routine in your classroom or in small groups. Whole-class investigations might result in shared writing (where the teacher does the writing and the students contribute through collaborative discussion) that gets posted in the classroom. Some investigations might be quick, spurred by a student question, and take place over only ten or fifteen minutes of class time (see Appendix G for some ideas). However, sometimes you'll want to provide opportunities for students to create projects or papers about their work. How do you move from research to writing? We offer some ideas here.

IDENTITY-FOCUSED NONFICTION WRITING

When we think about student writing projects, we start from a place of identity—who do we want our students to *be* and how will this particular writing project help them get there? This is a different starting point than many writing curricula take. We consider most writing curricula "product focused" because they often start with the question: What do we want our students to produce? (See Figures 8.1 and 8.2 for a comparison of the two approaches.)

Figure 8.1

Product-Focused Nonfiction Writing Unit	
Guiding Question (for the Teacher)	What will the students produce?
Answer	Specific genre or type of nonfiction writing
Possible Writing Products	Informational or argument/opinion essay, often similar to those that appear on standardized tests
Teaching Steps	• Read lots of examples of the genre/type of writing. • With the students, collaboratively identify main characteristics of this genre/text type. These characteristics often focus on form and structure of the writing. • Turn those main characteristics into a rubric or checklist. • Create scaffolds based on the rubric or the checklist (including graphic organizers, templates, sentence starters). • Select a topic for writing in the genre/type (ideally students have some say in the topic, but sometimes a class-wide topic is chosen). • Provide appropriate resources for research (often supplied by the teacher, sometimes acquired by the students independently or in small groups). • Ask students to produce writing and, ideally, receive feedback, revise, edit, and publish their work.

A product-focused writing curriculum is not in and of itself wrong. In fact, when this cycle of teaching is followed, a product-centered classroom can create good writers. Reading examples in the genre can be very helpful—think of the last time you had to write something unfamiliar; chances are you looked for an example! And students who have input in their rubrics tend to understand them better than when the criteria are handed down from the teacher or textbook. There are times when our students will need to produce particular written products, and the teaching steps outlined in Figure 8.1 will help them to do so. Even in an identity-focused classroom, you may move into this same product-focused cycle of teaching after students have completed some research and are ready to write.

However, in this book we offer a different vision for what information seeking and nonfiction writing can do for students. In this vision, we start from a different question, a question of identity.

Figure 8.2

Identity-Focused Nonfiction Writing Unit	
Guiding Question (for the Teacher)	Who do we want our students to *become* in relation to information and information seeking? How will this particular project help students in this becoming?
Answer	A specific goal or set of goals related to information seeking, handling multiple perspectives, evaluating information, and/or learning about expertise.
Possible Writing Products	Translational texts, including: • Picture books • Textbook entries for younger students • Wikipedia/encyclopedia pages • Blog posts • Newspaper articles • Letters to the editor • TED Talks • Podcasts • Museum displays • Pro/Con flyers • Cost–benefit analyses • Grant or project proposals • Nonfiction narrative
Teaching Steps	• Identify a topic, issue, or question to investigate (individually or as a whole class). • Assist students as they begin the process of investigation by identifying possible sources, including experts and stakeholders both online and in real life. • Demonstrate various ways of keeping track of information and determining where more information is needed. • At some point, have a discussion about product. You may do so at the beginning of the unit—select the genre/writing type specifically because of what that genre/writing type can do for student identity and growth—or after the students have found some information and can make a reasonable choice. • If necessary, look at some authentic examples of the product you are producing. • Collaboratively identify important characteristics of this genre/product with an emphasis on the translational features of the genre. • Guide students through the process of writing, revising, editing, and publishing their work.

TRANSLATIONAL TEXTS

We use the phrase *translational texts* to refer to the kinds of texts (including written as well as spoken and visual texts) that have the primary goal of helping the audience understand something. The writer is "translating" a complex topic or issue by making it accessible to the reader.

We believe that writing translational texts can assist students in deeply understanding their topic or problem. We've all had the experience of learning something better when we know we will have to explain it to someone else. However, our definition prioritizes *audience*—yes, the writer will come to understand the issue better, but the translation is ultimately for the benefit of the audience. In this way, our approach differs from such writing-to-learn strategies as RAFT (role, audience, format, topic) that also require translation on the part of the writer but do so only to help the student understand a concept (and share this understanding with the teacher, who already understood the topic to begin with). When one writes in a translational text, one is writing for someone who does not have a great deal of background on the topic or question. The audience is someone less knowledgeable about the topic than the writer.

As you can see in Figure 8.2, we consider many genres to be translational. Each genre has a different purpose for this translation—to inform, to explain, to persuade, to entertain—and each genre calls for a different level of expertise on the part of the author. In general, though, all have these features in common:

- The issue/topic is put into context—enough background information is provided to understand the information and its significance.

- The issue/topic is explained in language that is accessible to the audience. When the author uses specialized vocabulary, the words are defined in more everyday language.

- The author draws upon multiple resources to create the text. These resources may include multiple perspectives, types of expertise, or stakeholders.

Many translational genres also include these features:

- Controversies or uncertainties about the issue/topic are noted.
- The author attempts to generalize or categorize the topic/issue. Comparisons to other topics/issues may be used, or additional examples may be given.
- The author may speculate about implications, applications, or consequences of the issue/topic.
- Visual and/or multimodal elements accompany the written/oral text.

HELPING STUDENTS TO PRODUCE TRANSLATIONAL TEXTS

In a product-centered writing classroom, students are guided to produce an acceptable example of a particular product. The product is often broken down into its component parts, and students are supported as they produce these different parts and assemble them into a final product. Success is based on how well their writing conforms to the criteria established.

In an identity-centered classroom, students are supported as they engage in the research and writing associated with being a translator. Teachers support students to make sense of their topic/issue/question by doing the following:

- Accessing the appropriate sources to understand their topic (including both experts and stakeholders, if appropriate)
- Asking enough questions of their sources (including personal interviews) to understand the issue in terms of past (How did we get here?), present (What is happening now?), and future (What will or might happen next?)

- Understanding the necessary technical language, vocabulary words, and/or foundational concepts associated with their topic
- Answering the question: How big of a deal is this?
- Determining areas of uncertainty and areas of consensus around their topic/issue
- Selecting an appropriate genre or type of text to communicate their findings
- Drafting their writing to make their newfound knowledge accessible for others

Note that you *may* become product focused as you move from research to writing. Once students have engaged in the research process and selected a genre, you may do many of the same activities you would in a product-centered classroom—examine examples of the genre, determine some criteria for writing success (in addition to the translation success criteria above), provide some scaffolds for writing. However, the product is treated as *evidence* that the students are developing the identity of someone who cares about multiple sources of information, recognizes bias and perspectives, sees where information is uncertain and where it is settled, and so on. You may also be pleased to see spillover from your generalist teaching in other more curricular-centered research projects.

Ultimately, this is not a "writing" book, but we do believe students learn a great deal from writing—and from sharing their writing. They don't need to do this at the end of every investigation, but they should have some chances to do so within the course of a school year.

Characterizing Translational Texts

Review the list of translational texts in Figure 8.2 and choose one that you might like to try with your students. An alternative suggestion: let students see the list (or an abbreviated list) of translational texts and have them choose one. Look for examples of the text type online, read them carefully, and make a list of the essential characteristics. If you can, attempt your own version of the text with your information project. This will be a valuable model to be used in your own classroom.

Sharing What You've Learned

Find a colleague or a friend with whom you'd like to share the results of your project. If you've created your own translational text, share your product. If you would rather share without creating a formal product, do so—and use the experience to help you imagine how you might create less formal sharing opportunities in your own classroom (see Appendix G for more ideas).

Chapter 9

SELF-GUIDED COURSE: A FINAL WORD

Now that you've completed your own project, we hope you're filled with ideas for bringing generalist literacy into your classroom. As teachers, curriculum writers, and parents, we all want schools to help young people make informed decisions that will be useful as they face a future in which information access and assessment will be even more complicated. We know for sure that we cannot predict those future challenges with any degree of certainty. In the previous sections of this book, we have made the case for teaching generalist literacy in schools, arguing that it offers some preparation for the future, for life beyond school. We know that each of us—and each of our students—will surely encounter issues where we want or need more information. Sometimes these are issues we cannot escape, a health crisis, for instance, and sometimes the issues are born from a seemingly random curiosity, like why tennis ball cans pop when you open the lid. Sometimes the issues are in between a deep, personal need and a curiosity, for example, who we should vote for in the upcoming election.

So why generalist literacy instruction? Although there is a chance that it will help some students do better in their school subjects or set others on a new career path, the real reason is that generalist literacy will ultimately help us form a bridge between the student self and the adult self, that is, the adult self charged with taking care of ourselves, our loved ones, and our communities. In this sense, generalist literacy is, finally, a kind of personal literacy. As we are bombarded with opportunities to learn more—from the breaking news on our favorite media outlets to the tweets of influencers to everyday problems that need to be solved—we must decide what information we wish to pursue in what detail. In the end it may come down to this simple question: How big a deal is it? And the answer to that question is decided by individuals as they go about their everyday lives.

When you choose one entertainment option over another, you are saying that what I want most right now is total escape or excitement or intellectual stimulation. When you choose to contribute to one charity and not another, you are making a statement about what you believe is important. When you choose to sign a petition or vote or go to a chiropractor instead of an MD, you are making decisions. School can be a place where you learn to take the time to become informed about the decisions you make.

But here is the problem—in most instances the school day is organized around what the teacher (or school or state department of education) believes is important. Generalist literacy asks instead that you look for a sweet spot where you, the teacher, can find value in something your students see as important, something that is of interest or value to them. As teachers, we elevate or downplay classroom events and identify the choices at hand. What are the side effects of pushing one choice or another? Generalist literacy helps make your classroom a place that is relevant to the lives of students.

As you've made your way through your own project, we hope you've seen the value in this kind of instruction and are imagining ways to carve out time to bring the real world—your version of the real world *and* the real world of your students—into the school world.

All of us, young and old, are aware of the massive changes taking place as we try to gather and assess information. These changes result in new access and possibilities, but also new worries. What do most of us know, for example, about how the "personal assistant" that talks to us from our smartphone finds information? How prepared are we for the charts and infographics that are produced using "big data"? Countless new doorways appear to be opening, but in truth, we don't know where those doors lead. Our hope is that generalist literacy will prepare students for wherever that may be.

Part III

EXAMPLES FROM THE CLASSROOM

Generalist literacy is ultimately an identity—a way of being, knowing, and doing—that can be developed through activity. In Part III we explore what generalist literacy looks like across several classrooms. We encourage you to see these ideas as starting points for your own work. Because generalist literacy is designed to capitalize on student interest and concerns, the topics you choose to explore with your students may be different than the ones we present in this section. The topic itself matters much less than the dispositions, skills, and processes your students learn along the way.

In the pages that follow, you'll be introduced to a flexible instructional framework for creating units of study for generalist literacy instruction. We've illustrated this framework and the underlying instructional principles with examples from classrooms from across the country. However, generalist literacy need not wait for a formal unit of instruction. In the appendixes, you'll find resources for shorter activities and lessons, things that take from as little as five minutes up to a single class period. We included the following table to help you navigate the remainder of the book and find something that works for you, your students, and your curriculum.

<table>
<tr><th>If You Have . . .</th><th>Then Try . . .</th></tr>
<tr><td>A few minutes throughout the day or week</td><td>Generalist literacy routines, such as:<ul><li>Sharing your real-life questions and curiosities, as well as how you pursued answers</li><li>Making your go-to information sources public (e.g., the BBC, WebMD, the local paper) by referencing them as appropriate</li><li>Modeling the characteristics of curiosity, skepticism, and persistence in your own behavior—and labeling these qualities when you do</li></ul></td></tr>
<tr><td>Approximately ten minutes, once a week (or more frequently)</td><td>Designated weekly routines, such as:<ul><li>Read-aloud-think-alouds (RATAs), beginning with articles of your choosing, and then inviting students to bring in articles too (See Chapter 2.)</li><li>Headlines or local news reading (Pull up a good source of information and scan the headlines. If you have time, select and article to read aloud; this may turn into a RATA.)</li><li>Search-aloud-think-aloud (SATA) (See Chapter 3.)</li></ul></td></tr>
<tr><td>One class period at regular intervals (weekly/monthly)</td><td>Single, self-contained lessons, such as:<ul><li>Whole-class searching</li><li>Reading around the world (see Appendix E)</li></ul>Longer projects that can be broken into weekly sessions, such as:<ul><li>“Wonder projects” (Students explore an issue of their own choosing, with one day a week dedicated to reading and research. At the end of a designated time period—monthly, quarterly, semesterly—students share what they’ve learned with the class; see Appendix G for different sharing ideas.)</li></ul></td></tr>
<tr><td>One to four weeks</td><td>Short units of study that highlight generalist literacy practices</td></tr>
</table>

Chapter 10

PLANNING UNITS OF STUDY

We've created an instructional framework to help you think about how to foster generalist literacy through purposeful (but not prescriptive) activity. If you've ever been involved in setting up a workshop-centered writing classroom or an inquiry-based science curriculum, you may understand what we mean—these ways of thinking about curriculum include general principles with a lot of flexibility. Teachers can tailor a generalist literacy unit of study according to their contexts, grade level, curricular goals, student interests, and more.

When we think about curriculum, we think about three (equally important) components:

- The teacher
- The students
- The content

Although the content can be somewhat flexible (and somewhat unpredictable), in most generalist literacy units, the teacher and the students are following a fairly consistent set of steps.

THE TEACHER

The teacher is responsible for introducing the project and creating enthusiasm. Once the unit is underway, the teacher frequently models generalist literacy thinking and facilitates/scaffolds information seeking and synthesizing. The teacher also sets some time parameters on projects and helps students determine how to showcase or share their learning.

Teacher Steps in a Generalist Literacy Unit	
Teachers	**Possible Activities**
Determine an initiating activity/event that engages students and creates enthusiasm	• RATA of an engaging article (might be from a source you want the students to use, in a genre you plan to have the students try, and/or about a topic students will investigate) • Preparing for an upcoming field trip or class speaker • Personal story or anecdote from teacher • Issue or current event the students have been discussing
Introduce the project and parameters, including helping students make connections to the work and generate topic ideas	• Additional RATAs, with opportunities for students to ask questions or pitch topic ideas • Topic-generating activities, like brainstorming questions, making a list of what you like to do outside school, exploring intentional versus incidental information sources, thinking about the importance/preparation matrix, freewriting, reviewing headlines or current events or interest inventories (Some of these may be conducted with a partner or in small groups.) • Orienting activities (If the whole class is investigating the same topic, orienting activities may provide opportunities for making connections and generating ideas.)

Provide opportunities for students to get oriented and focus on a topic	• Inviting a guest speaker to provide general background (ideal when the whole class is researching similar topics) • Visiting to the library to "read around" • Reading tertiary sources (including Wikipedia) and using information gathered to generate more questions • Perusing a classroom book or magazine collection • Identifying a narrow topic that requires multiple sources of information to investigate well
Support students as they find, assess, and read sources	• Minilessons on credibility, perspective, expertise, and kinds of sources (Model using your own information-seeking project, or invite students to share their progress for the whole class to use as an example.) • Brainstorming kinds of expertise needed (each student creates their own chart) • Mapping sources on the landscape of information • Identifying and interviewing real experts (See Chapter 7.)
Scaffold synthesizing information	• One-on-one conferences with the teacher about research progress • Reviewing student research journals periodically • Projecting updates in small groups • Discussions around when to stop (when you've answered your question, are at a reasonable stopping point, and/or have decided you've exhausted your interest in the topic)
Explore the importance of visual representations (optional)	• Discussing the role of visuals (including photographs, infographics, graphs, artwork) in generalist literacy texts (See Appendix D.)
Create opportunities for sharing	Products (see Figure 8.2 for a list of translational texts) or other shared celebrations
Notes: For these generalist literacy units, many teachers have success putting students into small research support groups (three to four students) where students regularly check in with one another and provide feedback on progress. Remember to look for and celebrate the characteristics of expert generalists—curiosity, open-minded skepticism, persistence—as they naturally arise in the class.	

THE STUDENTS

Within a generalist literacy unit of instruction, students will undertake a process very similar to the one you completed in Part II of this book. You, as the teacher, will be scaffolding the process and helping students engage in metacognition about each step, but students must do the work for themselves. As you design your units of study, be sure students have an opportunity to participate in all stages of the process by using the checklist that follows.

A Teacher's Checklist for Generalist Literacy Unit Design	
Have I provided opportunities for students to . . .	Y/N
Personalize their learning by choosing their own topic and/or finding a connection to a topic I've introduced?	
Get oriented to an issue before being encouraged to narrow their focus?	
Identify and talk to a guide, if appropriate and feasible?	
Focus or narrow their attention to something manageable within the allotted time frame? Part of narrowing or focusing is helping students identify a topic that requires more than one source of information.	
Find and assess multiple, credible sources of information, including interviews (if appropriate and feasible)?	
Synthesize information while they are continuing to search?	
Determine when they are finished—when they've answered their initial question(s), are at a good stopping point, or have decided enough is enough?	
Share their learning in an authentic way?	

THE CONTENT

Content for generalist literacy typically comes from one of these places (or a combination): the curriculum, the teacher, or the students. In the pages that follow, you'll see five different units, each illustrating a different way of thinking about content. Some of the examples showcase what our journalist friends call "evergreen topics"—topics that are timely year in and year out, with new information constantly making its way into the public sphere. Evergreen topics may be tied to the curriculum or to the teacher's personal passions; we think of these units as somewhat more controlled because the teacher is able to select and preview good sources of information ahead of time. Creating a unit around an evergreen topic may be a good first step for early in the school year or for teachers working with younger students.

Other examples demonstrate how current events or student interests may drive generalist literacy units. These units are somewhat less predictable—when information is brand-new, it may change from day to day in ways that are hard to anticipate; when students are bringing in their own interests, the teacher may know less than the students. Yet these units most closely mimic what generalist literacy looks like outside of school or in the real world. The teachers we know who have embraced student choice and topic freedom report that students are highly engaged and that they themselves learn as much as their students do. The process is often energizing—for students *and* their teachers!

As you read about these generalist literacy units, consider what topics and products might work for your students. We hope you'll agree—the possibilities are nearly limitless.

Unit Title	Topic	Topic Source	Grade Level/ No. of Instructional Days	Product
Birds of a Feather	Making local birds "cool"	Teacher/evergreen	Upper elementary 10 days	Written and illustrated bird descriptions (individual)
Number Sense	Reading, interpreting, and creating numeric data representations	Curriculum/ evergreen topic	Upper elementary/ middle 8 days	Infographic
The Iron Horse Trail	Exploring the origins, construction, and uses of the trail behind the neighborhood school	Curriculum/ students	Upper elementary 15 days	Website and brochures for the community (collaborative) (A variety of other products were also inspired by the project.)
Who Am I?	Eighth-grader identity	Student/current events *or* evergreen topic	Middle 20 days	Formal product of student's choosing
Science Journalism for Teens	Current health-related issues	Student/current events *or* evergreen topic	Middle Flexible	Science news articles (individual or coauthored)

UNIT PLAN 1: BIRDS OF A FEATHER

In this unit, fifth graders produced a class book on birds native to their home state of Missouri. Their book, which also included beautiful student-created watercolors of each bird, became a treasured classroom resource.

Carrie Launius's primary goal was to introduce students to credible sources of information—what generalists consider "good starting points"—for their research, including *Science News for Students* and the online bird guide from the Cornell Lab of Ornithology (https://www.birds.cornell.edu/home/). Yet students also learned so much more: how to interview an expert, how to read for interesting facts, and how to compare information across sources. They also considered the role of illustrations and visuals in nonfiction texts.

This unit was successful in part because of Ms. Launius's enthusiasm for the topic—she loves birds! If birds aren't your thing, find something that is. Your enthusiasm will be contagious.

Day	Generalist Literacy Framework/Activity	Of Note
1	**INITIATING EVENT:** Perform RATA of an online article.	The unit starts out with a read-aloud of an article about elephants that will become a writing model and serves to introduce students to a great source of science information: *Science News for Students* (see Appendix C for annotated example).
2	**MAKE CONNECTIONS:** Introduce the project.	The topic—birds—is introduced through read-alouds of two books: *Project Puffin: How We Brought Puffins Back to Egg Rock* by Pete Salmansohn and Stephen W. Kress and *What Birds Do and Say* by Anne Kapler McCallum. The teacher's enthusiasm for birds is clear, but she also models noticing the "secret facts" authors include in their writing—the things that make birds so fascinating. By the time the teacher introduces the project at the end of class, students are eager to begin.
3	**GET ORIENTED, SELECT A TOPIC:** Explore classroom and online resources to select a topic.	Students use classroom and online resources, including the Ornithology Lab at Cornell University, to choose their own project topic—a bird native to Missouri. All students are working on the same type of topic, but no two have the same bird.
4	**GET ORIENTED, SCAFFOLD SYNTHESIZING:** Model the research and writing process.	Students are reminded of the goal—creating a publishable book chapter about their bird—and are introduced to another type of source, the interview. Together, they watch an online interview with an expert on birds. The teacher then models her own research process by finding "secret facts" about her own bird using the Cornell website. She then creates a rough draft on the spot.
5	**SOURCING:** Perform individual research.	Students use the sources they've learned about to begin their research—and use the research skills they've seen modeled to move beyond these sources.
6	**GET ORIENTED, SOURCING:** Prepare for an interview.	Students prepare to interview an ornithology professor from the local university by researching her background and using their own research to create questions as a class.
7	**GET ORIENTED, SOURCING:** Guest speaker, who also serves as a guide, visits.	The teacher uses student-generated questions to interview the professor (who visits the class in person). Students take notes, focused on why these birds live in *this* region.
8	**SCAFFOLD SYNTHESIZING:** Students work in writing/editing workshop.	Students work on writing their chapters of the class bird book. The teacher conferences with students individually and provides minilessons on common issues, all to advance the goal of publication.
9	**VISUAL REPRESENTATIONS:** Students illustrate the text.	Students produce watercolors of their birds.
10	**SHARING:** Celebrate!	The book is assembled, distributed, and read aloud during a class celebration.

QUESTIONS, CHALLENGES, AND EXPLANATIONS ABOUT THIS UNIT

Why this topic?

Although birds or local ecology may be part of the curriculum, the teacher began with birds to model how a personal interest should/could/might lead to research. So why birds? Although students were enthusiastic about becoming experts on their bird, they also understood that what they learned about research was ultimately more important.

Why begin with an article about an elephant? Why bring in books at all?

The teacher was following a powerful pattern of writing instruction: moving from whole to part to whole. She began by reading whole pieces of writing—an article and books—so that students could experience the power of coherent writing and have a mental model of what they would later be asked to produce. The fact that the article was about an elephant (and not a bird) didn't matter—the teacher was drawing the students' attention to how the author introduced facts and provided information about credibility within an engaging article.

Throughout the first two days of the unit, the teacher used the voices of skilled writers to create excitement and interest. She was also able to add to their storytelling by bringing her own insights and experiences to their foundation. Once the books had been introduced, the teacher pointed out some of the differences between books and websites (since the students would also be doing research with websites to create a book) and the importance of factual accuracy for both.

After introducing the expository whole (through articles and books), she moved the unit to the parts (collecting information) and then back to the whole (creating a class book of their own).

Why only one or two websites?

This may seem counterintuitive—isn't more usually better? Isn't choice a good thing? But we have learned over and over again that students need to see what an excellent site looks like before understanding why a poor one is, in fact, poor. The Cornell Ornithology site is not good simply because it's an educational site or because it is run by a prestigious university. Instead, it is good because of the research that it is based on and the way the information is organized and because it invites citizen scientists to participate. In short, it is highly informative and well curated. Once students became familiar with the Cornell Ornithology website, they could compare it to other sites and recognize what these websites did better, not as well, or differently.

Bottom line: we believe that it is better to begin any search by introducing students to great starting points (in the form of books, websites, or articles) rather than engaging them in search engine roulette.

Why watercolor painting?

This was a gamble that worked out beautifully. Students had never had an opportunity to work with watercolors in their regular class, and it made the project feel really special. Moreover, the watercolors allowed students to put information they had learned into visual as well as linguistic terms.

UNIT PLAN 2: NUMBER SENSE

This unit, originally taught with sixth-grade students, was designed to meet math and science standards related to representing data, interpreting graphs, and understanding statistics. It also incorporated an understanding of economics (required by many social studies standards).

The teacher's primary goal with this unit was for students to identify good online sources of numerical data, interpret the data, and represent their understanding visually. She achieved these goals by designing a unit around an evergreen topic in the city of St. Louis—baseball. Very few students in St. Louis are unaware of the importance of the local baseball team to the city, even if they aren't ardent fans themselves.

Within the broad topic of baseball, though, the teacher left plenty of room for topic flexibility—students had opportunities to look up numbers related to ticket sales, concessions, merchandise, as well as game statistics. Connecting all the topics under the umbrella of "baseball" simplified the beginning of the unit—where the teacher could harness the energy created by start of baseball season, nearly a local holiday in town—while still allowing for student choice once the parameters of the unit were established.

Day	Generalist Literacy Frame-work/Activity	Of Note
1	**INITIATING EVENT, MAKING CONNECTIONS:** The teacher, wearing a St. Louis Cardinals–themed outfit (sweatshirt, earrings, hat, necklace), announces the beginning of a new unit.	The teacher prepared a mostly visual PowerPoint covering various aspects of Major League Baseball. The slides showcase mascots, stadium design, logos, positions, and the structure of the playoffs. By the end of the class, all students have found a point of interest or connection to the business and/or game of baseball.
2–3	**GETTING ORIENTED:** Model the process of asking questions and looking for answers from credible sources.	Several relevant websites are introduced and discussed. For player statistics, students are introduced to team websites and taught how to calculate some of the basic player stats (batting average, earned run average). For economic data (e.g., player salaries, franchise value, impact on the local economy), the teacher compares the team sites to more neutral sources of information (e.g., newspapers, *Forbes*). The students practice asking questions and looking for relevant data on different sites.
4	**INTRODUCE THE PROJECT:** Students research and create an infographic about some aspect of baseball.	Infographics are a way of visually presenting numerical information and have become more prevalent in our visual culture. The teacher models a read-aloud with an infographic on hot dogs from four different ballparks. Students then practice reading infographics in small groups. By the end, students can explain what questions a particular infographic answers. They also begin thinking of their own infographic ideas.
5	**SOURCING AND SYNTHESIZING:** Choose topics and conduct research.	In pairs, students choose a baseball-related question that (1) could be answered through accessible data, (2) could be represented visually, and (3) would have enough different answers that the infographic could show differences (e.g., if all hot dogs were the same in cost and ingredients, there would be nothing to compare in the infographic discussed the previous day). Once topics are approved, students begin looking for data. Most start with the sources they've already learned about, but some need to find additional sources. How to evaluate sources for credibility is reviewed.
6–7	**SYNTHESIZING, VISUAL REPRESENTATIONS:** Determine the best way to represent information.	For this unit, the infographics are created by hand, using sketches. Students discuss how to represent their findings through such visual features as size proportion, color intensity, or position on the page. These will be presented and discussed as a whole class.
8	**SHARING:** Infographics are showcased and discussed.	When viewing each other's infographics, students write down their questions about the graphics.

QUESTIONS, CHALLENGES, AND EXPLANATIONS ABOUT THIS UNIT

How do infographics connect to statistics?

When you read an infographic, it appears that you are looking at factual information. And you may well be. But just because an infographic "looks" good doesn't mean it is a credible representation of data—and learning to critically analyze such visual representations of data is an important part of being able to interpret information in the twenty-first century. The underlying purpose of this unit is to help students realize that any visual representation is based on real numbers that have been collected from somewhere and layered with other numbers that have been collected in one or more places. Asking, "Who made this representation, and why?" and "What is included in this data, and what is missing?" is an important part of being data literate.

So might I do this kind of unit using another topic other than baseball?

Of course, but make sure that the sites that are used for building the infographic are reliable. For instance, there are really good health statistics available through the Centers for Disease Control. There is lots to compare just on that one site. For example, if asthma is an issue in your community, talk with students about what information they want to know about asthma. Model thoughtful question posing: Does asthma correlate to absenteeism in our school district? Are asthma rates higher in districts where coal production is also high? Is asthma more common in poorer neighborhoods? Even if students don't create an infographic, being able to pose good questions is a skill any generalist values.

Can't we just create criteria and have students find the sites?

The skill of identifying good sites is different from the skills involved in recognizing the qualities of a site and using it well. Schools often teach choosing and using sites as a linear process; first you come up with good terms to type into the search engine, and then you compare and assess what comes up on your screen. But we strongly believe that once individuals learn what a good site looks like and how to use it effectively, they will be better able to recognize other good sites that show up on whatever search engine they are using. With this in mind, help students by first identifying some useful sites where they can begin. Compare sites that you (or they) have identified and what those sites can or cannot offer. Then, by the time you get to the mechanics of the search engine, students will know more about what they are looking for.

UNIT PLAN 3: THE IRON HORSE TRAIL

This unit was designed by teacher and author Dr. Ruth Nathan to supplement a study of community life. Like many communities throughout the United States, the community's local railway route had been converted from a line of track to a path of dirt and blacktop that community members could enjoy. It was named the Iron Horse Trail. Student curiosity was high about how the trail had come about, and all the students were very interested in how everyone used the trail and what it meant to the community.

The teacher's primary focus was to develop the students' research and interviewing skills. Their curiosity was nothing short of an invitation! The research and interviewing skills the students learned in this unit served them throughout the year as they worked across the curriculum—from writing books and poems and larger research projects about nonfiction topics to biographical and autobiographical work.

Within the broad scope of the trail, there was plenty of room for topic flexibility: Where did the route begin and end? Why did it run through the town? When was it built? When did the trains stop coming? Why? Who thought of turning the track route into a path? How long did it take? Was anyone still living on the trail who was there when it was built? And so on.

Day	Generalist Literacy Framework/Activity	Of Note
1	**INITIATING EVENT:** Capitalize on student interest.	Prior to the unit beginning, the students discuss the trail and ask questions about it. To prepare for formal inquiry, the teacher makes certain that there is information available about the trail. The school and town library have plenty of information, as do various municipal offices and people living in homes abutting the path. The teacher writes students' questions on the whiteboard. After discussing these questions, she solicits more questions, and the class groups the questions by topic (e.g., questions about the original railroad, questions about how the idea for the trail came about).
2	**GETTING ORIENTED:** Students learn about the kinds of sources different questions require.	The teacher models the process of finding answers to different types of questions. She teaches students to consider what sources they might need to answer questions such as the following: What railroad ran through this town? How did the rails to trails project begin? Who uses the trail, and how?

3	**INTRODUCE THE TWO RELATED PROJECTS:** Two translational texts are introduced.	The final products are introduced: a website about the development of the trail and a brochure to place around the local community (e.g., office waiting rooms, community bulletin boards). Before class, the teacher prepared a PowerPoint showing different kinds of websites for the students to consider. She also shares approaches to writing brochures. The teacher allows students to browse the website and mentor texts without going into too much detail just yet.
4	**MAKE CONNECTIONS:** Topics are considered based on student interest; work groups are formed.	The teacher reminds students of the topics brainstormed on day 1—each topic includes a group of student-generated questions. Students apply to join one of the groups by writing their name on a sheet of paper and explaining why they chose their inquiry focus. Applications are separated and reviewed by the teacher before forming the topic groups.
5-8	**SOURCING AND SYNTHESIZING:** Group and individual research performed.	Members of each group gather information relevant to their topic. Working together, each group decides how their portion of the website should be organized. Groups also gather visuals to support their text. Many of the visuals are snapshots of primary sources gathered from community archives; some are graphs that are the result of interviews from both residents living on the trail, their relatives, and/or students currently attending the school.
9–10	**SYNTHESIZING AND SHARING:** First drafts are created.	Before groups begin creating their portion of the website, the teacher and class determine what components should go into each section. A website includes different types of writing (expository, persuasive, narrative, question and answer, etc.) and different modalities (pictures, video clips, audio files, etc.), and the class discusses what each group should include on their portion of the website. They strive for a sense of balance and coherence across sections of the website, while also determining how to best represent each group's research findings. For each component, they also develop criteria for evaluation (e.g., what makes an image "good"?). Finally, they discuss when and how to link from their new website to additional information available elsewhere on the web. Students begin writing drafts of their translational texts with the knowledge that this work is a recursive process. For example, groups may continue to read, check their sources for accuracy, and seek permissions where necessary even while drafting their product. When the first group finishes a rough draft, the teacher engages the class in a whole-group RATA of the page. This helps support student revision and provides a model for other groups.

(continues)

(continued)

Day	Generalist Literacy Framework/Activity	Of Note
11–12	SYNTHESIZING AND SHARING: Students confer with peers.	Students work on what they hope is their next-to-final draft and spend time on peer conferencing. For this activity, two small groups are paired together to exchange work. Students offer feedback on clarity, structure, mechanical correctness, and factual accuracy to members of another group. They also use the criteria the class developed on day 9 to assess the effectiveness of each component of the website. After receiving feedback, students return to their topic groups and revise as they deem appropriate.
13	SHARING AND CELEBRATING: The website is created and celebrated.	Students share their final drafts, and their work is then placed on the website by the teacher.
14	CONSOLIDATING AND SHARING: The second product is created.	The second product, a brochure, is shorter than the website. A template is created with headings for each of the group's topics (e.g., history, uses). Groups discuss how to pare down their information to fit in the allotted space. As they complete their work, they add it to the brochure template.
15	SHARING: The brochure is proofread.	The final brochure is printed, and groups review and proofread for mechanical correctness and factual accuracy. The final draft is printed, and copies are distributed locally.

QUESTIONS, CHALLENGES, AND EXPLANATIONS ABOUT THIS UNIT

How do you manage the process of groups working on different types of questions that require different types of resources and skills?

Although it is impossible to predict exactly what challenges will arise in a unit of exploration such as this one, strong classroom management and organization will support students (and teachers!) in this work. Consider explicit work and modeling around ways of listening and working in groups, collaboration, and approaches to peer conferencing, including listening intentionally and turn taking. This isn't the kind of project you can do at the beginning of the school year. Instead, it's something to build toward.

This kind of unit also requires a certain amount of preparation before its launch. For example, this unit required the teacher to investigate types of websites, choose the ones she felt the students could understand given their age, and prepare a PowerPoint with plenty of website examples. The nice thing is that because the PowerPoint was made, it was something she could share at a staff meeting and give to other teachers who were thinking about trying out this kind of unit.

What do you do when too many students are interested in one topic?

One topic can usually be divided into two. For example, many students wanted to explore how the idea for the trail developed. The teacher decided that this topic could be divided: one group would look into how this particular trail came about. The other group could research the development of other similar trails throughout the state. Was, for example, the Iron Horse Trail the first of its kind? (It was not.) The final entry on the website had two components: "Recreation Trails Come to California" and "The Iron Horse Trail Comes to Town."

What happens when the students don't want to stop?

Look for curricular flexibility—it's possible enthusiasm for your generalist literacy topic may be incorporated into the next unit of study. In the case of the Iron Horse Trail project, the class continued the exploration of the trail within a poetry unit on writing about place. The children wrote poems about how they felt about the trail, and those poems eventually were published on the back of a T-shirt, which was sold to parents, with the proceeds going to trail conservation and development.

UNIT PLAN 4: WHO AM I?

This unit was developed for the fourth quarter of eighth grade, a time of transition in many parts of the country as students graduate from middle school and move on to high school.

Prior to this unit, students in this class had plenty of opportunities to think about and practice generalist literacy skills. Throughout the year, their teacher engaged the class with many of the shorter activities mentioned in this book, including RATAs and whole-class searching. He regularly modeled his own generalist literacy dispositions and practices and encouraged students to do the same. In this unit, the teacher's goal was for students to further hone their generalist literacy identities while also celebrating this important time in their lives.

This unit is much less structured and predictable than earlier examples. Under the large umbrella of "my identity," students are given wide latitude to select a topic and determine how to share their findings. Because of all the freedom available to students, the teacher must be flexible and willing to adapt to unexpected questions, roadblocks, and topics. By the second week, students are arranged in research feedback groups of three to four for the remainder of the project. These groups are formed based on student topics and work preferences and serve as an important source of support for both the teacher and students. For example, students who are researching ancestry or cultural/ethnic background make up one group; those who choose to look into a hobby or sport that is important to their identity form another group (or set of groups); those who want to look into possible future careers are put together in their own group.

Because this project comes at the end of the year, it is sometimes interrupted by other end-of-the-year activities (including standardized testing, field trips, community projects, pep rallies, etc.). The unit is flexible, with lots of independent work time that can be tailored or adjusted as needed. Because it is focused on students' interest, this unit sustains their engagement, despite the many distractions that the end of the year presents.

Day	Generalist Literacy Framework/Activity	Of Note
1	**INITIATING EVENT, MAKE CONNECTIONS:** The teacher shares artifacts and photographs from their own life and encourages students to ask questions and make connections.	The unit starts with the teacher sharing memories about his life as a fourteen-year-old. Because this is the end of the school year, the class has developed a safe rapport, and the teacher feels comfortable sharing his embarrassing eighth-grade school picture, along with his taste in music and film from the mid-1990s. Although the conversation begins with the teacher's identity, he invites students to make connections, comparisons, and contrasts with their own lives. Students are invited to ask questions before they spend time freewriting about the question: Twenty years from now, when you look back on this time in your life, what do you want to remember about who you are now?
2	**MAKE CONNECTIONS, CONSIDER A TOPIC:** Introduce the project.	The project is introduced: the students will investigate a topic or set of questions inspired by their own identity. Topics can be related to culture, biography, family history, current interests/events, or practice-linked identities (gaming, sewing, hiking, writing, sports, etc.). The teacher models by brainstorming topics related to his current identity and shares topics previous students have selected. Students are given several options for thinking about the project: freewriting, talking with a partner, exploring their beginning-of-the-year autobiographical poems, and looking at last year's projects.
3	**GET ORIENTED, CONSIDER A TOPIC:** Topics are pitched and honed.	Students use their previous day's work to further explore possible topics. The first half of the class is dedicated to modeling topic selection with volunteers who "pitch" their idea in front of the whole class and receive teacher and classmate feedback. By the end of class, each student submits one to three possible topics and potential sources.
4	**GET ORIENTED, IDENTIFY GUIDES:** Possible community guides are identified.	The topic of guides is introduced, and students brainstorm possible guides for one another. By the end of class, students have identified multiple possible guides in the community, some of whom may also turn into sources for the project.
5	**GET ORIENTED:** Prepare for a panel of guest speakers.	The teacher informs the students about an upcoming guest speaker event, which includes community experts in the following areas (inspired by student topics): adolescent health/development, local history, Latinx cultural traditions, health and fitness, college sports, video game design, the local environment. Each small group of students is given the name of one of the speakers to research and create possible interview questions. After all class sections have completed the activity, the teacher compiles the questions into one set of questions per speaker.

(continues)

(continued)

Day	Generalist Literacy Framework/Activity	Of Note
6	**GET ORIENTED, SOURCING:** Finish preparing for speakers, and model research process.	In small groups, students review all the questions and star the most important (the teacher will order the questions and submit to the speakers ahead of time). The students brainstorm everything they remember about research and assessing credibility from the year. Students share their research topics. Using an example topic, the teacher leads the class in thinking about possible sources and models a search-aloud.
7	**GET ORIENTED:** A panel of guest speakers serves as guides.	The guest speaker event takes place in the school auditorium. For all the students to see the guests, a special eighth-grade-only presentation is arranged.* Three rounds of interviews occur, with students rotating to the speakers of their choice. The speakers use the students' questions as starting points. Students take notes on a handout with the questions listed and ask additional questions.
8	**GET ORIENTED, SOURCING:** Guest speaker information is shared, and group norms are established.	Class begins with a guest speaker debrief and then the teacher puts students into small groups for the remainder of the project. (Students are grouped based on topics and their previous work habits/styles. These groups will support one another for the remainder of the project.) Norms for group work are established and progress charts are introduced (see Appendix H). The remainder of class is work time.
9–12	**SOURCING AND SYNTHESIZING:** Independent research is performed with small-group support.	Each class period starts with group check-ins. In each group, students share their progress and set goals for the day. Class periods end with students completing a research progress chart. The teacher checks in with each student at least twice over the course of the four days. Minilessons on the following occur as necessary: • Finding sources • Assessing credibility • Comparing sources of information • Identifying perspective and bias
13	**SYNTHESIZING AND SHARING:** Translational products are introduced.	The teacher introduces the possibilities for final projects: a recorded TED Talk; a photo story with narration, a Pecha Kucha, a picture book, a magazine-style article, a library display with a reader's guide, or a museum display with viewing guide. For all possibilities, mentor text examples are provided. In small groups, the students browse the mentor texts and discuss how these texts highlight the characteristics of generalist literacy.
14	**SYNTHESIZING AND SHARING:** Criteria for translational texts are established.	The teacher leads a whole-class discussion on each of the possible project products and answers questions related to the criteria of each. Students choose a product to create and begin their work. If necessary, research is finalized.

Day	Generalist Literacy Framework/Activity	Of Note
15–17	**SYNTHESIZING AND SHARING:** Products are selected, and research ends.	Students work on their project products, providing feedback to one another in small groups. Minilessons with small groups on the following as necessary: • Video-recording tools • Choosing visuals • Writing like a journalist • Attributing sources
18	**SHARING:** Products are finalized and tested.	A final workday. All products are shared in small groups, and final peer feedback is provided. Products that require technology are tested so there are no last-minute surprises.
19–20	**SHARING:** Projects are shared and celebrated.	Half of the students present their projects on the first day and half on the second. The day begins with presenting students briefly introducing their project, and the remaining time is spent circulating to view projects and write feedback notes. Food and drinks are shared in celebration.

*In years when the schedule will not permit all students to attend a single speaker, the teacher has arranged for a rotating group of speakers to come throughout the day, with all interviews recorded and posted to the school's website.

QUESTIONS, CHALLENGES, AND EXPLANATIONS ABOUT THIS UNIT

How do you negotiate a classroom with students doing so many different projects? How do you help students find topics, guides, resources, and so on?

There are a lot of moving parts to negotiate! As you move along throughout the unit, always start by asking students to brainstorm ideas individually (they might be brainstorming topics, guides, ideas for sharing their thinking, whatever step you are on). Some students will have lots of ideas right away, and some may struggle with the brainstorming process. Once students have a few ideas on paper, start by approving the topics of students who are ready so they can continue working independently. Do this in a whole-group setting so that all students can hear each other's topics and your responses—students who are having trouble coming up with ideas will benefit from hearing what their classmates are thinking. Next, focus on the students who have common and easily addressed questions (you'll get a sense of who falls into which category pretty quickly). For example, one student may be trying to decide between two or three possible topics and will benefit from a few follow-up questions to help them make up their mind. Once again, do this in front of the remaining class so that everyone can benefit from hearing the discussion. Once you are down to only the students who are really stuck, you can focus your feedback and scaffolding much more individually, while those whose topics have been approved can begin work.

You may find it easier to keep track of progress with a clipboard or electronic notes. You may want to note things such as student topics, whether or not you've conferenced with a student, whether the student has found a guide, and whether the student has multiple sources. On days for independent work, you can use these notes to determine who to check in with first. You will also want your students to keep track of their own progress either in their research journals or through progress worksheets.

How do you decide if a topic is acceptable? Will the student find resources? Is the topic too big or too small?

The tendency of most teachers is to expand topics ("And you could also look into X or Y or Z"). With issues related to identity, the goal is to help students find something manageable. Think back to your own work in Section II and share your process for narrowing down a topic with students. Also find ways to take advantage of the fact that students will be presenting for one another—they are each other's audience. Develop response groups whose job it is to offer feedback and teach them how to give productive feedback. For instance, you might teach students to ask each other, "What part of this idea interested you most?" and describe their main takeaways from each other's projects.

Why the focus on guides?

One important skill of the generalist is to learn to talk with people who have expertise. When you teach generalist literacy, one goal is to help students learn how to answer their own questions or curiosities. They need to learn how to begin with excellent starting sites, books, or, in this case, people. Since a teacher cannot know or keep up with all of the interests presented by students, guides become extensions of the teacher. Good guides should know more than you do. Remember, an important goal of this project is to help young people talk with adults, especially those whom they see as more knowledgeable about their topics. This project also helps students learn to recognize community resources—guides are all around us, if we know where to look!

Why all of those genre choices for finished products?

This unit is noticeably less about product than research. By introducing learners to a wide variety of ways to present their learning, you are not only promoting student choice but also introducing students to the various ways generalist information can be presented. Maybe some students won't do a TED Talk, but now they at least know what one is. If a teacher wanted to focus more on the end product and wanted similar products, they would spend time introducing and analyzing the genre.

UNIT PLAN 5: SCIENCE JOURNALISM FOR STUDENTS

This final unit represents the most flexible structure of all. Dr. Buerger, a middle school science teacher in Louisville, Kentucky, fosters generalist literacy through science journalism. For years, Dr. Buerger has been a part of the SciJourn project, and her students regularly publish articles in *SciJourner*, an online science newsmagazine for teens (http://www.scijourner.org/).

Every year, Dr. Buerger approaches this project differently, depending on her curriculum, the school calendar, and the students in the class. Some years, she blocks out "two-week sprints" where students work on the project intensely for ten academic days (with follow-up days as needed). Other years, she finds her students get ahead in their regular study and she can let the project unfold over the course of a quarter or even a whole semester, using the two- or three-day breaks in between units as SciJourn time. She reports that students adapt just as well to the stop-and-start process as they do to a two-week sprint.

Dr. Buerger's students are required to research a science topic and many end up exploring health-related issues. She emphasizes three aspects of generalist literacy: (1) knowing credible starting points for research, (2) accessing experts (all her students are required to contact an expert as part of their research process, and many get personal emails in reply!), and (3) persistence. Over the course of this unit, students work individually or with a partner to research and write a publishable article. Prior to beginning the project, Dr. Buerger also models generalist literacy extensively, primarily through regular RATAs and by expressing her own curiosity, skepticism, and persistence.

This project unfolds in the order depicted in the table that follows, but because of Dr. Buerger's flexible approach, it is impossible to divide the unit into clear "days of instruction."

Generalist Literacy Framework/Activity	Of Note
INITIATING EVENT: Read published work from previous students.	Many students are already aware that writing an article for *SciJourner* will be a project during eighth-grade science. Articles published by previous years' students decorate the hallways, and the teacher has engaged in many RATAs from the SciJourn website. The teacher introduces the assignment by having table groups read previously published articles and discuss what the students notice. Because students have already heard many RATAs, the teacher is able to direct their attention to the following: How does the author make the topic relevant and interesting for teens? What sources of information does the author use?
MAKE CONNECTIONS, GET ORIENTED, FIND A TOPIC: Good topics are discovered through brainstorming and reading.	In pairs or table groups, students brainstorm ideas they may be interested in learning more about. They also access sources of general science information, especially *Science News for Students* (https://www.sciencenewsforstudents.org/), to get oriented to the world of science journalism and to look for topics that pique their interest. Students are also encouraged to use tertiary sources to get background information before beginning a focused search. Students may work with a partner on the project. All partners must sign a contract outlining their responsibilities to one another.
SOURCING: Good sources of science information are introduced.	Because this is a science classroom, the teacher wants students to learn about credible sources of scientific information. She engages students in an activity about credible sources in which groups of students look up science acronyms like EPA, NIH, CDC, and NOAA and present the organizations to the class. These organizations become part of a good starting points anchor chart in the room. Throughout the unit, websites are added to the chart as the students encounter them.
SOURCING: Experts are contacted, using professional emails.	All students are required to email an expert with questions about their topics. Students research their expert first and then use a template to send a professional email (see Appendix I).
SOURCING, SYNTHESIZING: Multiple perspectives are sought and incorporated.	The teacher conducts minilessons on topics such as: • Finding multiple sources • Attributing sources appropriately • Explaining information in an accessible way • Getting a reader's attention
SYNTHESIZING: Journalistic articles are written.	Students write and receive feedback on multiple drafts of their project. The teacher reviews student work regularly and provides oral feedback—students often only need a quick comment to get back to work. Peer feedback is also a regular part of the process. Students have mentor texts from previous years to use as models, and they work together to support one another. The teacher also builds in regular graded checkpoints.
SHARING: Articles are submitted for publication.	Students send their articles to *SciJourner* for possible publication. The editor of *SciJourner* often requests additional revisions, which are completed outside of class time.

QUESTIONS, CHALLENGES, AND EXPLANATIONS ABOUT THIS UNIT

How do you keep from getting pulled in too many directions?

Even when the classroom appears a bit chaotic, students are generally making progress. They just aren't all working at the same rate. Some students might be researching, some typing, and some discussing their ideas with others.

One way to keep up with all the different student needs is to rely on other students in the room for help. If you are working from a laptop cart, for example, appoint a student committee to pass out and pick up computers. Designate go-to people for computer issues and other students who can help with instructions or issues with the project itself. This project also works best with peer review—because students are working toward authentic publication, they generally take this feedback very seriously and help others improve their work. In addition, being proactive as a teacher and setting up expectations that include possible hiccups for the day really helps avoid confusion.

How do you teach persistence?

Students love to collaborate, so it is important to emphasize sharing their work with one another. Ask students to show each other work in progress and problem-solve as a group when someone senses a roadblock. There is a fine line between struggle and total frustration. Let students flail some before "saving" them—students will feel more successful in the end and will develop important confidence and critical thinking skills. Offer tips or suggestions, but let the work be the student's own.

This sounds like a lot of work—why do it?

Students acquire skills and confidence from this unit. Perhaps as important, students who choose their own topics and persist in publishing their work report a sense of joy and accomplishment. This is true preparation for lifelong generalist thinking!

Appendixes

APPENDIX A
THE CURIOSITY SHELF

Somewhere in your classroom, find a place to display interesting objects that might inspire curiosity in students. Start with objects from your own life—natural objects found in your yard or on a trip or engineered objects (antiques are great). Eventually invite students to add objects from their lives too.

Keep sticky notes or note cards near the shelf for students to write down questions about the objects. Or, when you have time, take an object off the shelf and lead a class discussion about it. Let students handle the object and encourage curiosity and question posing. Questions might include:

- What's the function of this object?
- How old is this?
- What is it made from?
- Where did it come from?
- Who used this?

Help students think about how to answer their questions. Where could they go for help?

Note: Angela once facilitated a workshop for teachers in which a guest speaker brought in an array of objects to illustrate the research process. Small groups looked at objects like an antique nail remover and the leather glove of an Olympic hammer thrower. Each group had a limited amount of time to figure out what their object was, using any available resources (including the Internet). Participants found themselves on patent office websites, poring through Google images, and querying other teachers in the room. The teachers had a great time—and they found themselves honing their curiosity and their research skills!

APPENDIX B
STUDENT SURVEY: GENERALIST LITERACY

Read each statement and circle the appropriate response.

Thank you for your responses!

SA: strongly agree
A: agree
D: disagree
SD: strongly disagree
N: no opinion

		SA	A	D	SD	N
1.	Learning is boring.					
2.	I learn best by reading books and answering questions.					
3.	As I learn, I find myself asking lots of questions.					
4.	I learn more if I have a choice in what I will be learning.					
5.	I learn more when I talk things over with a partner.					
6.	I learn more when I work in a small group and share ideas.					
7.	Discovering answers to my questions is interesting.					
8.	The best way for my teacher to give me a grade is for me to take tests.					
9.	A good way for my teacher to give me a grade would be to talk with me, read my journal, or watch me as I work.					
10.	I like to talk about things that interest me.					
11.	Learning is finding out about things that interest me.					
12.	Learning about science is only important and fun for kids who are good at school.					
13.	I enjoy reading books from the library about real people, places, and things.					

		SA	A	D	SD	N
14.	**I spend time on the Internet checking what others tell me is true.**					
15.	**I spend more time searching on the Internet than reading books.**					
16.	**Reading science textbooks is the best way to learn about science.**					
17.	**I can learn more by doing something than reading about it.**					
18.	**I can remember facts that I discover by myself better than facts someone tells me.**					
19.	**I think about where information comes from.**					

List three to five topics you would like to know more about.

APPENDIX C
READ-ALOUD-THINK-ALOUD: AN ANNOTATED EXAMPLE

Following is an annotated example of a read-aloud-think-aloud (RATA) conducted by Ms. Launius with her fifth-grade students. Ms. Launius read this article on the first day of their unit investigating birds native to their state. Her goals with this RATA were to introduce students to the website *Science News for Students* (https://www.sciencenewsforstudents.org/), to provide an example of a well-written science story about animals that they could use later as a mentor text for their own writing, and to demonstrate the following generalist's skills and dispositions: identifying perspectives and sources in an article, opening multiple tabs, monitoring comprehension, and understanding the role of visuals.

We've embedded Ms. Launius's "Think Alouds" in the article that follows so you can see where she paused and voiced her own thinking process, along with our own commentary to help you follow along.

> Ms. Launius has opened this website before class begins. Before she begins reading, she says: "I came across this really interesting article that I wanted to share with you all. This article is in a magazine I like, called Science News for Students—the same organization also publishes a magazine called Science News. I love these magazines because they're written to help people learn about new scientific discoveries. Science News for Students is free to access for everybody—I hope you'll start looking at it regularly too."

If you think your students will need more information about why *Science News for Students* is a good source of information, you can also show them how to look for the sponsoring organization at the bottom of the website—Society for Science and the Public—and then look that organization up in Wikipedia. The organization has been around since 1922, has a mission to promote an understanding of and appreciation for science, and sponsors various science fairs and competitions. Though you may not wish to go into so much detail every time you access a source, modeling how you know a source is good is necessary from time to time—and not only for websites that aren't credible. Accessing this information will also allow you to recognize the potential perspective of this article—*Science News for Students* has the editorial perspective that science is exciting and important. She then skips past the photograph and begins reading.

After telling the students why she likes this source, Ms. Launius begins by reading the title and the subtitle, then saying, "I wonder what they mean by 'low, low rumble' . . . guess we'll find out." She then skips past the photograph and begins reading.

* * *

Elephant Songs

Scientists figure out how elephants make their low, low rumble

Elephants sometimes communicate with sounds below the range of human ears. Researchers recently found that air rushing through the larynx can create the superlow sounds. Photograph credit: katja from Pixabay

By **Stephen Ornes**
Aug 20, 2012—5:13 PM EST

Elephants are well known for their trumpet-like sounds, but they can "sing" superlow songs, too. You'll never hear these tunes in full, though. That's because elephant songs include notes too low for the human ear to hear.

"Hmm, that's interesting. I always think of noises being too high to hear—like a dog whistle." Several students nod.

Ms. Launius compares the information in this sentence to something she (and many students) already know about, showing how she makes connections.

Some scientists had suggested that elephants make these low sounds in the same way that cats purr—by squeezing muscles near the voice box, or larynx.

"Ooh, that word *had* tells me maybe they learned something new. Like, they used to think one thing and now they don't."

But elephants don't need to use throat muscles to go low, say scientists in a new study published in the journal *Science.*

"Yep!"

Such ultralow sound frequencies are known as "infrasonic" notes, or "infrasound." The sounds can travel as far as 10 kilometers (6.6 miles) in the air. (For comparison, the song notes audible to humans travel only about 800 meters through air.) The superlow songs may also vibrate the ground, sending infrasonic signals even farther. The researchers mimicked the lowest part of the song by blowing air through the larynx of an elephant that had died. The experiment showed that just rushing air passing through the larynx makes the fundamental sound of the song.

"These numbers seem interesting, but I'm not sure I understand them. I'll come back to this."

With this finding, "there's no need to go into the purring hypothesis," Christian Herbst told *Science News.* Herbst, a voice scientist at the University of Vienna in Austria, worked on the new study of elephant song. (A hypothesis is a possible explanation that gets tested during a scientific experiment.)

"So they did find something new—a new idea that changes the way scientists used to think. And this guy, Christian Herbst, is someone who worked on the experiment. That's great—this reporter did some work and interviewed the scientist. But I'm pretty sure this scientist would think this idea is a big deal since he did it, right? I wonder what other people think."

Ms. Launius models recognizing the strengths and limits of expertise.

An elephant's larynx works like those in people. It's like a tunnel with strips of tissue, called vocal folds, across it. Air traveling from the lungs through the larynx separates the folds. Then they come back together and create puffs of air.

"Think of a flag in the wind," Herbst told *Science News.*

"Okay, this helps me understand how it works. I'm remembering last week when the wind was blowing so hard and the flag was making a lot of noise." Students are nodding. "But the flag's noises were just one sound. How would it get higher or lower?"

That process leads to the formation of sounds. Larger folds mean lower sounds, and an elephant's vocal folds are eight times as large as a human's. If people had larger vocal folds, we could speak in lower tones—and possibly even communicate in infrasonic voices.

"Okay, I think I get it."

The quest to explain elephant sounds doesn't lead to easy experiments. When it comes to an elephant's sound production, "We really do not know that much," Peter Wrege from Cornell University in Ithaca, N.Y., told Science News. Wrege, who studies animal behavior but did not work on the new study, runs a project that uses infrasound to keep track of elephants in the forests of Central Africa.

"Hey, look! They did talk to someone else. This guy also sounds like an expert—I know Cornell is a good university, and it sounds like he studies elephants too—but because he didn't work on this study I kind of trust his opinion on whether this is important news. I wish he had said what he thought about this idea about the larynx, though."

Herbst knows firsthand how hard it is to probe sound production. For his own experiments, he's put equipment into his mouth to study his own voice. But that wouldn't work with big animals, he said.

"The elephant would just close his mouth and say, 'Thank you for the snack.'"

Ms. Launius notices that the article includes multiple perspectives but also suggests a limitation to the article. Remember, no source will ever be perfect.

"Okay, ha ha." The students smile. "I'm still wondering about the distances. So, I know that 800 meters—the distance humans can hear—is two laps around a track, but how far away is that?" She opens up another tab in her browser and demonstrates converting meters to miles using the calculator available on Google. "About half a mile. Can anyone think of something a half a mile away?" A few students suggest places, and Ms. Launius uses Google maps to confirm. They find a gas station about a half mile away. "So we can hear sounds that far. Pretty far. But how far did it say elephants can hear?" She demonstrates returning to the previous tab. "I'm glad I kept this article open. It makes it easier to go back and forth. Six point six miles. Wow. Can anyone think of somewhere that's 6.6 miles away?" Once again students provide suggestions, and Ms. Launius uses the map to identify a place. They determine that another elementary school is approximately 6.6 miles away. "Wow—that's really far! Can you imagine if we could hear them out on the playground every day?"

Ms. Launius demonstrates how to use various search tools and how to think carefully about information presented to be sure she understand.

* * *

Ms. Launius doesn't talk about the image until she's finished reading the article. When she returns to it, the following dialogue occurs:

Ms. Launius: Let's look at this picture for a moment. Do you think this picture is a good match for the article?

Student 1: Yes! It has elephants!

Student 2: But it's about elephants' singing, not just about elephants.

Ms. Launius: Does the picture help you understand the story?

Students: Kind of. Yes. Not really.

Ms. Launius: For those who said yes, why?

Student 3: It helps me picture what an elephant looks like. I like it.

Ms. Launius: Yes, it does. If you had never seen an elephant, this would be helpful. For those who said no, or not really, why?

Student 2: I think a picture of an elephant larynx would help more. Or maybe a map showing how far you can hear the sound. Something else. But maybe you could have the picture of the elephants too.

[Several students nod.]

Ms. Launius: I see what you mean. I think of this picture mostly as decoration. Other pictures might be more helpful, but this one is not a terrible match for the story. It just doesn't really teach us anything more.

Because Ms. Launius was using this RATA to help students get ready for a project in which they would write about an animal, the lesson concluded with the students talking about what made this article interesting to read. Depending on your purpose, you may conclude your RATAs simply by ending your reading and transitioning to the rest of the day's work, or you might reinforce something you really want to highlight in the article (credibility, perspective, etc.). You might also end by having students list questions that the article inspired—you could have students look up answers right away or simply save the questions for another time.

APPENDIX D
THINKING ABOUT VISUALS

The role of images and other multimodal elements in informational and nonfiction texts has expanded dramatically in recent years. As you lead read-aloud-think-alouds (RATAs) and share texts with students, don't forget about the visuals that accompany these texts. The most basic question to consider is this: What is the function of this image/visual/multimodal element in this text?

The image might:

- **Serve as decoration:** We consider a visual to be "decorative" when it is only superficially related to the content included in the rest of the text. The image/visual is there to add visual appeal or to create an aesthetic impression. The photograph that accompanies the article "Elephant Songs" in *Science News for Students* (see Appendix C) is an example of a decorative image. The picture is of elephants walking in a line, and the article is about the biology that enables elephants to communicate over long distances.

  Some decorative/aesthetic images may also communicate **tone or perspective** in ways that the printed text does not. For example, a close-up image of a dolphin swimming through plastic-strewn waters is quite different from an image of a beach taken from a great distance. Both images may appear as decoration next to an article about a particular method of cleaning ocean waters, but they send quite different messages about the severity of the problem. As you engage in RATAs, you may wish to choose some articles that have decorative visuals that attempt to communicate perspective.

- **Repeat information in another mode:** Images may also serve to repeat or reinforce information already communicated via the printed word. For example, many science textbooks have visuals that accompany printed information (a diagram of a cell, for example, next to a paragraph defining "cell membrane" and "nucleus"). Photographs may also repeat information—in a *New York Times* article about tornadoes, pictures of downed trees and destroyed homes might accompany a paragraph explaining the damage.

Note that whenever information is communicated in a different mode—when you turn words into a diagram, for example—*information is gained and information is lost.* In other words, images and printed words can never be completely redundant to one another, even if that is the author's intent. Semiotician Gunther Kress (2005) often uses the example of a cell diagram. As soon as you attempt to draw a cell, you have to make a lot of decisions that you don't have to make with the printed word. Where exactly does the nucleus go? How big is it? How far from the edge of the cell? All of these decisions may or may not be important to meaning. Similarly, when a book is turned into a film, many visual decisions must be made about things the book leaves up to the reader's imagination. Angela often uses the example of Harry Potter books and movies. In the movies, the director had to cast *all* of the students in Hogwarts, not just the characters who were described in the books. Each person cast has a gender, race, ethnicity, height, weight, and so on that the viewer sees and may attach importance to.

- **Add information not communicated in the printed text:** Visuals may also communicate information not found anywhere else in the text. For example, the kiddle.co entry "Diabetes Mellitus Facts for Kids" (Kiddle 2019) has several images, a graph, and even a short video. Each of these visuals adds more information that is not available via only the printed words. Many of these visual and multimodal images require specific skills to understand, skills that students may not acquire without explicit instruction. Though math and science teachers are generally quite comfortable teaching students to read traditional graphs and literacy teachers are generally acquainted with helping students unpack images in picture books or in film, the complexity of the visual landscape continues to expand. An infographic, for example, is often a complex mix of visual and statistical information. We've found that the best way to support students in this ever-changing environment is to engage in RATAs with visuals frequently—and show your own thinking process, especially when you are confused.

- **Not have anything to do with the printed text at all:** Finally, remember that in an online environment, the visuals on your screen may not have been designed to accompany the text you're reading. The visuals might be part of advertisements or sponsored content. Visuals might accompany clickbait to drive you to another website, or they might accompany links to other articles within the same publication. For those of us who are comfortable with the online environment, this may seem obvious, but we have seen students attempt to use unrelated visuals as supportive tools for making sense of an online text. If you are reading an article with a lot of distracting and unrelated visuals aloud to your class, explain how you know not to become distracted by those visuals. Students will benefit from hearing about the clues you use.

Many resources exist for thinking about visual and multimodal texts with students. If this is an area that interests you, seek out more resources. The National Association for Media Literacy Education (namle.net) may be a good starting point.

APPENDIX E
READING ACROSS GEOGRAPHY

One of Angela's colleagues—an excellent generalist—once said, "I never read current events or political news from only one country. I always read across geography." She is multilingual and has the advantage of being able to read the newspapers in several languages, but even if your students speak only English you can "read across geography." Many English-language newspapers are published all over the world (see list at end for possibilities).

To demonstrate how geography influences perspective, try one of the following activities:

1. Start with a trusted source of information that you have already discussed with your students—the BBC, the *New York Times*, the *Washington Post*, or the *Wall Street Journal* are all possibilities. Choose one of the top stories and facilitate a read-aloud-think-aloud, focusing specifically on how the author puts the issue into context and discusses the importance of it. (If you select the article ahead of time, you may also want to prepare printed copies of the article for students to refer to.) Assign each small group a different news source to access, and ask students to look up this same issue on their news source. Each group should take notes on the similarities and differences between the articles, and students present their findings to the rest of the class. Students should also look at how important the topic appears to be visually—where in the paper does it sit? Is there a photo?

2. Assign small groups a different news source to access. Ask them to read and take notes on one of the main news stories in their source. Each group should present their story to the rest of the class while you take notes on the board. Lead a discussion about the differences you see in what each source chooses as a main news story.

Notice that there is no need for activity other than discussion. This activity is designed to acquaint kids with the concept of reading globally and how to go about it.

Following is a list of sample possible news sources:

United States (national papers)

- The *New York Times* (www.nytimes.com)
- The *Washington Post* (www.washingtonpost.com)
- The *Wall Street Journal* (www.wsj.com)

England/United Kingdom

- The BBC (www.bbc.com)
- The *Guardian* (www.theguardian.com)

Russia

- The *Moscow Times* (www.themoscowtimes.com)

China

- *China Daily* (www.chinadaily.com.cn)

The Middle East

- *Al Jazeera* (headquartered in Qatar) (www.aljazeera.com)
- The *Daily Star* (Lebanon) (www.dailystar.com.lb)
- *Haaretz* (Israel) (www.haaretz.com)
- *Hurriyet Daily News* (Turkey) (www.hurriyetdailynews.com)
- The *Jerusalem Post* (Israel) (www.jpost.com)
- The *Jordan Times* (Jordan) (www.jordantimes.com)
- *Tehran Times* (Iran) (www.tehrantimes.com)

Many U.S. newspapers provide low-cost or free digital subscriptions to educators. Libraries also often have access to digital news sources. Work with your school or public library to find more!

APPENDIX F
WHOLE-GROUP INTERVIEW EXAMPLE

In Webster Groves, Missouri (just outside of St. Louis), a park is named in honor of Ivory Crockett. Students in one elementary classroom wondered who Ivory Crockett was. The teacher happened to know a lot about Mr. Crockett—and had even met him on several occasions. She thought he might be willing to come talk to her students, but rather than just invite him in as a guest speaker, she decided to use this opportunity to help her students develop interviewing skills.

For the teacher, Mr. Crockett was a perfect candidate to interview because:

- He was someone the teacher knew and had access to. (*Accessible*)
- He had excelled in an area of student interest (sports). (*Interesting*)
- His claim to fame was questioned—student thinking would be needed to make sense of the controversy. (*Promotes information digging*)
- As an African American champion who was successful, outgoing, and open, he made an excellent choice. (*Model*)

To prepare for the interview, students followed the steps listed in Chapter 7, including reading Wikipedia, accessing additional sources, and brainstorming questions. They also read short biographies about a variety of different people and talked about how the author may have found each piece of interesting information—what questions did the author ask to learn each piece of information? Students also discussed the purpose of the interview they were about to conduct—why bring Mr. Crockett into class when they could read so much about him online and in other sources? Together, they decided they really wanted to know more from his perspective. How did he feel about his accomplishments? What was his life like? Who supported him along the way?

After the class brainstormed questions together, small groups sorted the questions and eliminated redundancies. The students decided that, rather than the teacher asking all the questions, they would divide the final list of questions among student volunteers. Their final list is shown here. Notice their last question!

- What was it like when you were young? Tell us about growing up.
- Who was your greatest support growing up?
- Did you participate in other sports besides running? Did you excel in them?
- What motivated you to learn to run so fast?
- How did your coaches support you mentally and physically?
- How did you train before you broke the record?
- What did you think about while you were running? What did it feel like when you got the nine-second time?
- How did you feel when you didn't qualify for the Olympics?
- Did you ever experience racism during your time racing?
- How did it feel to be an African American track runner at that time?
- Do you wish that more people knew about your accomplishments?
- As you reflect on your life, what might you change?
- How does winning the world record influence your life today? How would life be different if you didn't hold this record?
- What advice would you give kids today who want to become a professional athlete?
- Is there anything else you would like to share with us?

After the interview, the students all wrote Mr. Crockett a thank-you note and used their newfound knowledge of Mr. Crockett and interviewing for their next class project.

APPENDIX G
IDEAS FOR SHORT/ INFORMAL SHARING

When students don't produce formal projects, papers, or presentations about their work, they'll still want to share what they've learned. Here are some ideas that require little or no outside preparation:

THE THREE-MINUTE REPORT

This kind of sharing is best done in small groups and often grows out of a read-aloud-think-aloud (RATA). After a RATA (or after a particularly enthusiastic classroom discussion), ask students to generate follow-up questions. What are they wondering? What do they want to know more about? Put students into small groups and have them look for answers to one question (or set of questions). After ten minutes, give each group three minutes to report on their search process and what they learned. In your follow-up questions, highlight their generalist literacy practices—curiosity, persistence, skepticism, sourcing, getting oriented, and more.

CAROUSEL CONVERSATIONS, ROUNDTABLES, OR ELEVATOR SPEECHES

These formats can all work as ways to share information at the end of a small or a large project. After students have had a chance to investigate a topic or issue of their choosing, ask each student to create a chart like the following:

<table>
<tr><td colspan="3">Topic/Question:</td></tr>
<tr><td>Type of Expertise Accessed</td><td>Source</td><td>Key Facts/ Information</td></tr>
<tr><td></td><td></td><td></td></tr>
<tr><td></td><td></td><td></td></tr>
<tr><td></td><td></td><td></td></tr>
<tr><td></td><td></td><td></td></tr>
<tr><td></td><td></td><td></td></tr>
<tr><td colspan="3">Additional Questions (If Any):</td></tr>
</table>

These charts can form the basis for sharing. Try one of these formats:

- **Carousel conversations:** Collect all the charts from the previous day and divide the papers into four to five groups (you might group the projects thematically, according to feedback group, or randomly). On the day you plan to share, post the charts in clusters around the room. Divide the class into groups of three or four and give each group a pack of sticky notes to use to write feedback (if possible, each group can have different-colored sticky notes). Allow the groups to rotate around the room to examine all the charts. At each stop, they should write at least one note on each project. After groups have rotated around the room, return charts to their creators and engage in a whole-class discussion. *This allows every student to look at every other student's project.*

- **Roundtables:** Divide the class into small roundtable groups of four or five students each. If students have been working in research feedback groups during the length of a project, be sure to mix up the groups for roundtable sharing. Explain that a roundtable is one way that researchers share their work at professional conferences—and roundtables are best for sharing and getting feedback on work that hasn't been written as a formal paper. Each student should get five minutes to explain their project and key findings, followed by two minutes for the rest of the group to ask questions. *In roundtables, students will only hear about the projects of their small group. This allows for more detailed sharing.*

- **Elevator speeches:** Explain that an elevator speech is named for the amount of time it takes to ride the elevator to a top of a building—less than one minute. Give the students time to look over their charts and practice a one-minute (or less) speech explaining the most important thing they learned about (1) their topic and (2) searching for information. Provide a chart for the audience to use to take notes during the elevator speeches. Afterward, you may want to provide time for students to mingle and follow up with one other on their questions. *This allows students to hear from all of their classmates in a very short amount of time. It also requires students to deliver a very succinct speech in front of the whole class.*

"JUST THE FACTS" SLIDESHOWS

Each student is allowed a single slide to present the key information learned during an investigation (if the project is longer, consider allotting two or more slides), along with the source of information and type of expertise the source represents. Depending on your students' topics, you may want students to focus on the most interesting or unusual facts, the most important facts, or the most controversial/debated information. Compile all the slides into a single slideshow and present it to the class. You might have students give short speeches to go along with the slides, or you might play the slideshow automatically and require the words to speak for themselves.

A FINAL NOTE ON SHARING: DON'T FORGET TO RECOGNIZE WHEN ENOUGH IS ENOUGH

In our information age, it's possible to spend hours (or days or weeks) investigating a topic. This is great—and we want to encourage our students to be persistent and dig for information beyond the superficial—but not all topics need to be investigated so deeply. What sounded like a fascinating topic or question when you started may turn out to be not so interesting after all—and part of living in the information age is knowing when to stop. Whatever projects your students do and however you choose to have them share their learning, leave space to talk about what it means to be finished. Did you answer all your questions, or did you decide to save some for another day? Did you decide this wasn't so interesting, or did your topic take you in a new direction? What might you do next (answering "nothing" is sometimes okay!)?

APPENDIX H PROGRESS CHART

When students are working independently on a project, you may want to scaffold their work time. Either in their research notebooks, on a worksheet, or in an online document, have students fill out the following:

At the Beginning of Class (Be Sure to Refer to Yesterday's Chart, If Applicable)	
Today's Goal 1	
Today's Goal 2	
Today's Goal 3	
At the End of Class	
Main Accomplishment	
Questions/ Roadblocks	
Support I Need from the Teacher	
Where I Will Start Next Class	

Model how to set reasonable goals based on the amount of assigned work time—it may be helpful for students to discuss their goals with their small groups at the beginning of class. Flip through student charts after class to keep track of progress and design whole-class and small-group minilessons.

APPENDIX I
ADVICE FOR EMAILING EXPERTS

Of all the teachers we've worked with, Dr. Marsha Buerger is the best at helping her students get responses from real experts. Here's her advice:

> I require all students to attempt emailing a researcher or expert for more in-depth information on the topic they are researching. At first, I thought this would be an exercise in frustration. I honestly didn't think busy professionals would take the emails seriously and respond. However, I was pleased and surprised when PhDs and MDs from prestigious learning institutions not only replied but replied with enthusiasm!
>
> Several issues developed as the students were working on their emails. The first was that they wanted to ask broad, nonspecific questions such as: "Tell me all about your research" or "What is your research about?" We had to have a minilesson on how to write two or three specific questions that showed the researcher that the students had read their work, were specific, and would not take an enormous amount of time to answer.
>
> The other issue was the amount of time it was taking to conference with students and suggest corrections to the rough drafts of their emails. This was really holding up their progress. The solution was to provide them with the following template where it was much easier for them to fill in the missing information, list two to three questions, and get it sent off. When students receive a reply, the excitement level in the room just explodes with clapping and cheers and provides an authentic experience to their writing.
>
> I believe that we received so many replies because the emails had a few specific questions and that the researchers were surprised that students were taking the time to write to them. If and when the students were published, they would send the link to the person who helped them, and they usually received a very positive response. In fact, one professor asked for a picture of the students: he put up a copy of the article and the students' picture in the hallway of the university!

EMAIL TEMPLATE

Dear Dr./Professor ________________________________,

Hello! My name is ________________________________ and my partner's name is ________________________________. We are students from [school] in [state] and are writing a science news article for SciJourner.org—a National Science Foundation–funded project. We are very interested in the research that you did about [research topic]. If you are not too busy, we were wondering if you could answer a few questions for us to include in our article.

1.

2.

3.

If we get published, we will email you back and let you know! Thank you so much for your time.

[student signature]

REFERENCES

Achieve the Core. www.achievethecore.org.

Adam, Hajo, and Adam D. Galinsky. 2012. "Enclothed Cognition." *Journal of Experimental and Social Psychology* 48: 918–925.

BBC. "Space." BBC.com/earth/tags/space.

Bruner, Jerome. 1976. *The Process of Education*. Cambridge, MA: Harvard University Press.

Caulfield, Mike. 2017. "How News Literacy Gets the Web Wrong." *Hapgood.* https://hapgood.us/2017/03/04/how-news-literacy-gets-the-web-wrong/

Central Intelligence Agency. "The World Factbook." https://www.cia.gov/library/publications/the-world-factbook/.

Cole, Joanna, and Wendy Saul. 1996. *On the Bus with Joanna Cole: A Creative Autobiography*. Portsmouth, NH: Heinemann.

Engel, Susan. 2015. *The Hungry Mind: The Origins of Curiosity in Children*. Cambridge, MA: Harvard University Press.

Freire, Paulo. 1985. "Reading the World and Reading the Word: An Interview with Paulo Freire." *Language Arts, 62*(1), 15–21.

Illinois Library. n.d. "The Information Cycle." https://www.library.illinois.edu/ugl/howdoi/informationcycle/.

Janks, Hilary. 2018. "Texts, Identities, and Ethics: Critical Literacy in a Post-Truth World." *Journal of Adolescent and Adult Literacy* 62: 95-99.

Kiddle. 2019. "Diabetes Mellitus Facts for Kids." https://kids.kiddle.co/Diabetes_mellitus.

Kohnen, Angela M., and E. Wendy Saul. 2018. "Information Literacy in the Internet Age: Making Space for Students' Intentional and Incidental Knowledge." *Journal of Adolescent and Adult Literacy* 61: 671–679.

Kress, Gunther. 2005. "Gains and Losses: New Forms of Texts, Knowledge, and Learning." *Computers and Composition* 22:5–22.

McCallum, Anne Kapler. 2017. *What Birds Do and Say: An Orinthological Primer for the Young and Young at Heart.* Alpharetta, GA: Lanier Press.

Moll, Amanti, Neff, and Gonzalez, 1992. "Funds of Knowledge for Teaching: Using a Qualitative Approach to Connect Homes and Classrooms." *Theory into Practice, 31*, 2, 132–141.

Mumford, Lewis. 1961. *The City in History*. New York: Harcourt.

Pearce, Charles R. 1999. *Nurturing Inquiry: Real Science for the Elementary Classroom*. Portsmouth, NH: Heinemann.

Salmansohn, Pete, and Stephen W. Kress. 2003. *Project Puffin: How We Brought Puffins Back to Egg Rock*. Gardiner, ME: Tilbury House Publishers. Updated version available: https://www.amazon.com/Project-Puffin-Improbable-Beloved-Seabird/dp/0300219792/ref=sr_1_1?keywords=puffins+kress+egg+rock&qid=1576167564&sr=8-1.

Saul, Wendy, Angela M. Kohnen, Alan Newman, and Laura Pearce. 2012. *Front-Page Science: Engaging Teens in Science Literacy*. Arlington, VA: NSTA Press.

The Merriam-Webster.com Dictionary, Merriam-Webster Inc., https://www.merriam-webster.com/dictionary/curious.

Thomm, Eva, and Rainer Bromme. 2012. "It Should at Least Seem Scientific!" Textual Features of 'Scientificness' and Their Impact on Lay Assessments of Online Information." *Science Education, 96*(2), 187–211.

Wineburg, Sam, and Sarah McGrew. 2019. "Lateral Reading and the Nature of Expertise: Reading Less and Learning More When Evaluating Digital Information." *Teachers College Record, 121*(11).

Index

A

B

C

R

S

W